A New Imagining

Towards an Australian Spirituality

Tony Kelly

COLLINS DOVE
Melbourne Australia

Published by Collins Dove
A Division of HarperCollins*Publishers* (Australia) Pty Ltd
22–24 Joseph Street
North Blackburn, Victoria 3130

First published 1990
Reprinted 1991
Designed by Jennifer Richardson
Cover design by Jennifer Richardson
Cover illustration by Jennifer Richardson

Typeset in Bitstream Charter by Collins Dove Desktop Typesetting
Printed in Australia by Griffin Press Limited, Marion Road, Netley,
South Australia

The National Library of Australia
Cataloguing-in-Publication Data:

Kelly, Anthony, 1938–
  A new imagining.

  ISBN 0 85924 828 3.

  1. Sociology, Christian—Australia.
  2. Australia—Religious life and customs.
  I. Title.

261

Acknowledgements
Our thanks go to those who have given us permission to reproduce
copyright material in this book. Particular sources of print material
are acknowledged in the text.
Every effort has been made to contact the copyright holders of text
material. The editor and publisher apologise in those cases where
this has proved impossible.

To my mother and father,
and to all who have struggled
to hand on what is best,
to allow the new to happen.

Foreword

For several years now, many of us have been dreaming of a better Australia. We have had the strong feeling that Australia might—very seriously—be in search of its soul. We who are Christian have dared to hope that this search would be conducted in the light of the Gospel.

A few years ago, I wrote that 'the Australian quest is varyingly expressed, as the search for a purpose, the search for a centre, the search for a heart'.

I pointed out then that 'Australia is what it is today because of the choices it has made'. Each past choice now presents a challenge: which choices will we now make to shape our future? In many areas we need to chose anew if Australia is to realise its true potential.

In May 1985, the Australian Catholic Theological Association noted 'we find ourselves in the midst of a culture still in the making, and thus we may still have a unique opportunity to contribute to its formation'.

I am pleased that Father Tony Kelly has decided to make a further contribution with this book.

I have always thought of Tony Kelly as a poetic theologian. There is nothing more real than true poetry. There is nothing more poetic that the theology of God's Word working through all that is good and true and beautiful in our created world.

In this book, *A New Imagining*, Tony Kelly sets forth some of his insights into the ways in which, in today's Australia, we might discover anew both the wonder and the challenge of God's gifts. 'Bicentenary Australia,' he writes, 'has invited a retelling of the Australian story.' There are times when the Spirit stirs in a number of individuals with the same prophetic restlessness. Reading Tony's retelling, I felt the same movement of the Spirit that breathes in Eric Bogle's bicentenary song:

> *The future was ours to protect, to proclaim,*
> *Paradise lost or Paradise gained.*
> *And tell me:*
> *Is Paradise here—after two hundred years?*
>
> *Beneath the Southern Cross*
> *It's time to tally up the cost,*
> *What we've gained and what we've lost—*
> *forever.*
> *Though much has gone we can't replace,*
> *Those of us who love this place*
> *Together now must turn and face*
> *the future...*

Tony Kelly develops those same themes more fully. He suggests some ways in which we might 'stumble towards what we might yet become', owning the past, acknowledging present reality, facing the future with hope.

We can do this all the more confidently if we share the age-old vision of the Christian faith and bring to it 'a new imagining', the 'bolder imagination' of Christian hope, the 'more compassionate imagining' of Christian charity.

Basic Christian virtues need to be alive and working within our Australian context:

> *Faith is always the promise of a new beginning: in place of the world as absurd, it cultivates a gracious vision of ultimate love and providence. The hope that it inspires is not defeated by despair over failure, past or present. The charity it inspires demands forgiveness of past wrongs and self-forgetfulness in moving forward into a future from which no one may be excluded.*

There are many of us who share Tony's conviction that 'the genuine Australia is still to be formed', that 'new issues of national integrity are still to be faced'. We share, too, his belief in 'the possibility of another kind of Australia..., not just a natural habitat but a human place'. We hope for healing, we believe in the possibility of better things.

We would share his conviction that it is not the narrow-minded politician nor the materialistic businessman who will lead us.

Rather it is the serious song-writer, the theologian who, with poetic imagining, does his own Dreaming. It is the average Australian who will allow his or her mind to open out to newness. Tony Kelly's book will help us to do this, inviting us to a 'spirituality which is essentially intelligence alive to the wonder and mystery which cannot be suppressed without mutilating the deepest sense of self. It frees consciousness from the superficial, the absurd, the tragically alienated, into a sense of the dynamic interrelated whole'.

Spirituality (which this book is all about) is an exciting and poetic reality:

> ...being in touch with the real questions of life as they arise out of our most genuine sufferings and, for that matter, our most precious joys. It is the centre where we do not surrender to some lesser version of ourselves, where we break out of all the 'little boxes', speak with our own voice, or keep our own silence, rather than follow the scripts that others have prepared for us. It is the challenge of finding the real centre and the ultimate connection.

I am honoured that, by means of this foreword, I am once again associated with a respected colleague in search of the harmony between God's grace and the wonders of his world.

I am grateful to Tony Kelly for this book. I am sure that many will find it heartening and enlightening. And 'those who love this place' will feel that Fr Tony Kelly has helped us to make a significant step towards the creation of the Australia we wish to see.

Bishop E. J. Cuskelly M.S.C.
Auxiliary Bishop
25th May, 1989.

Contents

Foreword   vii
Introduction   xi
1. Soul in Silence   1
2. Talking Points and Embarrassed Silences   25
3. Having a Heart   35
4. The Australian Conversation   62
5. Imagining Our Past   90
6. The Land Held Holy   103
7. Their Place   110
8. Australian Mysticism   118

Introduction

The 'new imagining' I am attempting here is, I realise, a rather odd project. For it is neither theology, nor philosophy, nor spirituality in any traditional sense, let alone a work of cultural or literary criticism in the academic mode. Still, there is room for a reflection on where we are as Australians which attempts to combine elements of different ways of thinking about what is most meaningful in our lives. If I have to settle on one word, it is 'spirituality', but, as you will see, I acknowledge its relative usefulness, and keep stretching it into other frames of reference.

Ideally, any publisher would say I should have this kind of thing ready for the Bicentenary. But being a year late, you do have an advantage. So much varied and high-grade reflection on our cultural situation has appeared with the 'Bi' in mind.[1] It is a resource to be used for those of us, who, more dilatory in coming to the celebration, now have the leisure to ponder the questions that are emerging. Having lived one quarter of our bicentenary history, some of that time overseas in Europe, Asia and North America, I have become slowly awake to the uniqueness of our Australian situation. Though we are finding ourselves, I think, in a time of cultural and social crisis, there is a still grace to be found; a new beginning, a new imagining.

These reflections began to take some kind of shape in 1988. In May, I gave a lecture on 'The Inarticulate Heart' sponsored by the Brisbane Catholic Education Office; and then, a couple of months later, a series of talks in Sydney for the annual conference of The Australian Association for Religious Education, at St Joseph's College. Out of these efforts came the general idea for this book, and I remain grateful to those who forced me to think about the deeper matters of the Australian heart and soul. The original setting of these reflections was in the context of religious education. This comes through rather obviously in what I have written. The education issue is a recurring theme, as you will see.

But in doing this I realised that I was drawing on other wisdom. If there is one name I should mention it is that of Peter Malone. I cannot think of anyone in Australia who has stimulated more thought on Australian spirituality than he. As editor of *Compass Theology Review*, he has drawn together some of our best thinkers and writers on Australian religion, culture, art and theology. He is probably better known for his specialised writings on films, but as editor, or 'co-ordinator' as he terms himself in a recent collection of essays, his contribution cannot be passed over.[2] Without his work on this theme over the last ten years, I doubt that I would have had much to say, or considered it a worthwhile theme.

Further, I have used the writings of the late Bernard Lonergan, a Canadian Jesuit, one of the truly seminal thinkers of our time, to make a number of points. Other Australians have extended Lonergan's writings into spirituality. Frank Fletcher and John Bathersby (now Catholic Bishop of Cairns) have done this far more learnedly than I. However, I thought there were applications to be made within an Australian context; and I have attempted some of them in a way that I hope will be both challenging and useful for further conversation around the deep matters of soul and heart that no human being, let alone Australians, can fittingly avoid.

A further resource has been Les Murray's *Anthology of Australian Religious Poetry*.[3] The many poems I have cited are almost all to be found in this remarkable collection. Further, Murray's own perceptive comments on this book and on Australian culture generally have often been points of inspiration in my own explorations. You could say this book is written as a response to the *Anthology...*, even though I heartily reject any notion of replacing such an inspired collection of high-quality poetry with my own laboured prose. There is just enough of the poet in me to enable me to appreciate the occasions when others have said it better. That is why I have tended to cite our poets and other writers rather extensively.

When I entitled this little book, *A New Imagining*, I was delighted to find in a recent work of one of our most imaginative Australian theologians, Denis Edwards (*Called to be Church in Australia*), a quotation from David Malouf's *The Sun in Winter*. A Belgian woman is talking to a young Australian visitor in Bruges:

> 'To see what all this really was,' she insisted '—beyond the relics and the old-fashioned horrors and shows—you needed a passion for the everyday.' That was how she put it. 'And for that, mere looking got you nowhere. All you see then,' she told him, 'is what catches the eye, the odd thing, the unusual. But to see what is common, that is the difficult thing, don't you think? For that we need imagination, and there is never enough of it—never, never enough.'[4]

When, in my *A New Imagining*, I try to suggest the moral, intellectual, political and historical forms of imagining the world 'otherwise', I am taking imagination in a broader sense. But there is a family resemblance to what the Belgian lady is saying; and her words remain very apposite to what this book is about.

What is it about then? The following chapters will tell. Still, the title of a fine poem by Noel Rowe, an Australian priest-poet, serves to encapsulate what these pages will explore. It is 'The Structure of the Real',

> ...The structure of the real
> is mercy. Having seen so many reversals,
> I should have known he would test his muscles
> on the stone, and walk away from the dazed
> grave, leaving its mouth open and amazed.[5]

How we Australians can imagine 'the structure of the real' in more gracious and healing forms is the concern of our 'new imagining'. How the resources of Christian faith can find fresh imaginative forms to serve this larger imagining is an ever-present question to me throughout my reflections. And how our education systems can be a schooling in such imagining seems to me to be the crucial issue.

1. Two recent examples are John Rickard, *Australia: A Cultural History*, Longman, London and New York, 1988; and John Fiske, Bob Hodge, Graeme Turner, *Myths of Oz; Reading Australian Popular Culture*, Allen and Unwin, Sydney, 1987.

2. Peter Malone (ed.), *Discovering Australian Theology*, St. Paul Publications: Homebush, 1988. Hereafter, *Discovering...*

3. Les Murray, *Anthology of Australian Religious Poetry*, Collins Dove: Melbourne, 1986. Hereafter, *Anthology...*

4. Quoted in Denis Edwards, *Called to be Church in Australia*, St Paul Publications, Homebush, 1988, p. 40.

5. *Anthology...*, p. 146. 'The Structure of the Real', © Noel Rowe, was first published by *Quadrant* in December 1985.

Chapter 1: Soul in Silence

For it is as Australians that we relate to one another, understand ourselves and interpret our world. As Australians we confess whatever faith we have and experience in our hearts the judgment of God. Our land with all its beauty, bounty and menace, gives our souls symbols for prayer. It is here that we find the presence of grace, or drift further toward an antipodean hell.[1]

opposite region

Australian?

There is no small problem in setting oneself the task of speaking about Australian spirituality, however tentative such ambitions might be. You soon come up against an enormous irony. The two key words are easy targets for those suspicious of airy abstractions. First, who could or should speak about *Australian* spirituality? It sounds like some kind of defensive nationalist concentration precisely at a time when global concerns are most urgent. For what was peculiar to particular places and times is rapidly yielding to a global culture. This is being brought about by the mass media, instant communication, massive migration. The developments are intensified by the need to respond to the global scale of what threatens humanity in the ecological crisis, in the growing world poverty, and in the possibility of thermo-nuclear self-destruction.

For 'Australian' to be featured in any description of culture or spirituality would be about as appropriate, so it appears, as to talk about feeding the world's hungry by farming kangaroos. Australia is involved, like it or not, in this emerging stage of planetary history. Though our small population does in fact occupy a continent, it is generally viewed from 'over there' as a huge national park rather than as a hotbed of the culturally significant and spiritually deep.

So, an *Australian* spirituality? Is it not all too late for such 'Down Under' reflections. To persist in keeping such a nationalist adjective looks more like a symptom of nationalist narcissism rather than a contribution to what is happening on the globe. True, there is a certain international interest in Australia as a kind of last frontier with its attendant 'flavour of the month' emphasis, so well typified in *Crocodile Dundee, Young Einstein* and so on. But why take ourselves so seriously? Some Australians do not find that we are a particularly likeable nation![2]

Indeed, taking ourselves too seriously would, I think, be rather un-Australian to start with. Still, why not take ourselves as we are? It is true we are not the repositories of the world's wisdom. We are not the home of one of the world's classic cultures, the way Europe, India, China, perhaps North America, might be. Yet there is no common humanity worth striving for if it is merely the emergence of a 'standard humanity' a version of 'mass man' in modern technological culture. For today we know something about ecology; and that includes the ecology of human culture. We are quite justified in being conservationist in regard to ourselves. Only in that way can we offer to the larger consciousness of human history our unique witness. For there is a uniqueness in living on this continent. Here, Easter is in autumn and Christmas is in summer, and the South wind blows cold. Here, our two centuries of European occupation, with all their inauspicious and tragic beginnings, are being awkwardly confronted by the uncounted millennia of Aboriginal pre-history. And now, like it nor not, we are increasingly in contact with the ancient worlds of Asia.

So, this 'Down Under' experience has its own point of view. It is not as though we are merely excavating for fossils in the way we might unearth the bones of the giant kangaroos or wombats that once roamed the land. Our singular experience is not of purely palaeontological interest. For our history has not finished. Very evidently, it is going forward into a new stage, perhaps to fizzle as an experiment that failed, perhaps to die into something more wonderful and more healing than what we have known.

An Antipodean Viewpoint

The distinctiveness of the Australian point of view has been perceptively remarked upon by Nicholas Jose.[3] Apparently curious things happen to the great issues of humanity when they are spoken of in this country. Two paradoxes make up this distinctiveness:

> 'The first is that the fundamental problems of mankind are rapidly transmuted to local questions. Who are we? What are we doing here? In Australia such questions have a particular meaning and relevance apart from their wider metaphysical significance. They are inevitably tied up with questions about national identity, and the distinctiveness of existence in Australia, as if the larger questions cannot be answered without first answering the more socially specific questions: who are we Australians and what are we doing here? Perennial philosophical questions raise particular anxieties in Australians, and Australians tend to respond to the general issues of the time in idiosyncratic and particularised ways . Worldwide discussion on nuclear disarmament, for example, is reflected in Australia chiefly through the dispute over whether Australia should export uranium mined from land to which Aborigines have sacred claims. Australians have their own angle of viewing universal concerns of our species and the larger movements of world history, and the angle has to do with being Australian. Australian sceptics suspect that universals, world trends, international crises and the like are only so as seen from Europe or North America.[4]

For good or for ill, the larger human questions do not get much attention unless they are posed in a manner that chimes in with our 'Down Under' experience. They need to come home to us in a particular way.

european cultures brought in the richness

q

'...Australians have inherited an odd way of thinking about them-selves. Towards the end of the eighteenth century, an ancient fantasy of the European mind was actualised in The Great South Land, which from the start acted out the ambivalent expectations of the antipodes. Its exotic flora and fauna were obligingly topsy-turvy by old-world lights. It was an uninhabitable waste yet the chance of a fresh start, a place of monstrous forms but of strange virgin beauty, a last paradise but also the antithesis of all that was civilised. It was the world upside down, a recognition that survives in its commonest nickname: Down Under...Whatever else one may say about Australians, they take pride in being an "odd lot", set apart. If they do not claim superiority, they hold ironically or defensively tight to their uniqueness. It is not an exportable com-modity.[5]

On the positive side, however much we may be an 'odd lot' or a 'weird mob', such an observation points to our feeling that we do have a contribution to make to the larger scene. There is an Australian angle; the view from 'Down Under' does offer a genuine perspective. In an unusually inarticulate way, we sense that being Australian belongs to the integrity of what we are as human beings. Compared to 'over there', it is neither superior nor inferior. It is not going to replace the classical efforts of philosophy or theology in exploring the human condition. Simply, matter of factly, it is experience of reality from where we are. And, of course, after a couple of centuries of cultural tutelage from 'over there', we are now unusually well positioned to spot that the versions of the human condi-tion we have received are very much British, French, German, Italian, North American expressions in ways their authors do not often realise.   Still, we may as well face up to the negative possibilities in our paradoxical situation. The implicit distinc-tiveness of our point of view can stunt our global perceptions:

'That leads to the second paradox. From the Australian point of view, the great issues of humanity can easily look like someone else's problem. The point is not intended flippantly. Whatever else Australian thinkers and writers may do, whatever world problems they may engage with, their work also has a separate Australian purpose. They are writing and thinking Australia.[6]

The ambiguity of talking about Australian spirituality is thus nicely made. The issue constantly challenging us in not only 'writing and thinking' but in praying, acting and imaginatively forming Australia, is not to lock ourselves into a traffic jam on a one-way street, it is to be open to a two-way flow of traffic and exchange. A healthy irony is the saving grace here. That will be what most powers a wholesome national imagination. If we think of ourselves as involved in a great planetary conversation celebrating all the richness of our world's particular histories, there seems to be no reason not to make our distinctive contribution, and so to increase our global sensibilities in the process.

Our Interesting Experiment

While 'Australia' is only a fragment of human history, it is where, what and why we are. It *is* something; something never tried before; at least an interesting experiment. Perhaps, as time goes on, it will emerge as a crucial experiment. It could be important, the way one national history in this world, and one continent in its geography, might make room for a more complete human experience. It is a matter of raising our awareness of how, on a global scene, we can both receive and give.

In short, despite the international influences and pressures of the present, there is no need to write ourselves off as an extinct species from the beginning. The 'survival of the fittest' was a model for the romantic capitalist mind of the First Enlightenment. A larger human responsibility has begun to question this. Too many have been left out as casualties of such progress. And many of us now are not prepared to be uncritically part of it. The issue is not the survival of the fittest in unlimited progress, but how our future can allow for the emergence of a more human world. In the context of such a challenge, we need what has often already been called a 'second enlightenment'. For this stresses the values of mutual belonging in contrast to self-promoting independence. It tries to imagine how differences can be respected, promoted, celebrated, rather than flattened into uniformity by the technological steam roller. Even a little insect can be important in the ecology of the billabong: without it, the setting sun would see no Brolgas dance!

Spirituality?

This second term, *spirituality*, presents a more serious problem to Australians. If *Australian* presents at least a terminological problem to the spiritually aware in today's world, *spirituality* encounters tough resistance in the Australian understanding of things. True, it is not such a good word, resonating rather too abstractly and prettily to communicate something about real life and radical imagination. It does not immediately connote the patience and creativity required to imagine the world otherwise. It does not conjure up the sense of protest on behalf of our real selves against oppressive collective versions. It tends to signify a retiring from the real world rather than an active, compassionate immersion in it. It suggests an isolated sensitive individuality rather than a universal belonging—almost a self-centredness at the expense of self-transcendence into the real centre of things. While not a good word, it is difficult to find a better one. Given the general pragmatism of our cast of mind, the very oddness of 'spirituality' can evoke a sense of that part of ourselves which is too often repressed or disowned. Even if we want to get on with the job, it is worth pondering the aphorism: 'Profound self-recollectedness [is] in fact the condition of noble activity.'[7]

A Spiritual Imagination

There is another, more activist way to look at it. It amounts to cultivating a special kind of imagination. In this sense, it is an awareness that calls into question the flat, dead images of routine life: 'imagination is the irrepressible revolutionist' (Wallace Stevens). Most of all it resists that modern kind of corrosive pessimism that leads to paralysis rather than to the release of creative energies. To this degree, spirituality is about where we radically stand, and where we move to from that point: 'the slow fuse of the possible is lit by the imagination' (Emily Dickinson).

But what kind of imagination? As Richard Kearney has pointed out, such creative imagination has to be at once ethical and poetic.[8] As ethical, it resists being drawn into a social communication of masks and images, and keeps looking for a face, especially the face of the suffering other. In such eye-to-eye contact with one's fellow sufferers, it is a response to the questions: Where are you? Where do you stand? 'We find in the face that haunts the imagination the ethical demand to imagine the world otherwise.'[9] 'Beyond the image, the face resides: the face of the other who will never let the imagination be.'[10]

However, if such an ethical imagination is not to degenerate into censorious moralism of the 'Wowser' variety, it must also give full expression to its poetical potential. It needs to play. Kearney makes a shrewdly profound observation:

> *'...one might even say it needs to play because it is ethical—to ensure it is ethical in a liberating way, in a way that animates and enlarges our response to the other rather than cloistering us off in a dour moralism of resentment and recrimination.'*[11]

Indeed, such a spiritual imagination 'needs to be able to laugh with the other as well as to suffer'.[12] In such laughter and compassion, it begins to imagine the world as it could be otherwise. From there it goes on to form its strategies of resistance for the sake of a larger human wholeness.[13] It becomes, eventually, political.

Hence, a spirituality, embodied in creative and subversive imagination, is what these reflections are about. We can take the matter further.

Patrick White, with characteristic trenchancy, expresses his belief in the need for spiritual integrity:

> *'I believe that most people hunger after spirituality, even if their hunger remains in many cases unconscious. If those who dragoon us ignore that longing of the human psyche, they are running a great risk. The sense of real purpose, the life force, could be expelled from a society whose leaders are obsessed by money, muscle, machinery. That society could—quite simply—die.'*[14]

White recognises the 'dragooning' forces of a culture addicted to wealth, power and technology . A massive 'something else' imposes social roles, writes our scripts, alienates us from the genuine depth and breadth of human life. White acknowledges that hunger for something more might be in many cases 'unconscious'. Yet without a larger vision, a sense of life's shared mystery, we are all dead.

Living our Questions

Such spirituality is not a fully expressed faith. Still, it is the condition for the flourishing and radiance of such a faith. Without it, a religious faith is a series of strangely coded answers to unasked questions. It has been said that there is nothing so ridiculous as the answer to an unasked question. When a question is not lived, even the most compelling answer is irrelevant. That, I think, is the fundamental meaning of spirituality : being in touch with the real questions of life as they arise out of our most genuine sufferings and, for that matter, our most precious joys. It is the centre where we do not surrender to some lesser version of ourselves, where we break out of all the 'little boxes', speak with our own voice or keep our own silence, rather than follow the scripts that others have prepared for us. It is the challenge of finding the real centre and the ultimate connection.

Traditionally, religion, philosophy and art are the sources and expressions of such spirituality. Today there is evidence of other dimensions of such a search. Psychology and social concern point to a further depth and breadth. The more personalist psychologies of Jung, Frankl, Rank, Rogers, Maslow disclose the depth of human consciousness, while those who most try to change dehumanising structures soon discover that at issue is how human beings are critically imagining their possible community.

Reserve?

You might think that this is very intense stuff, ballooning out in all kinds of inflated terms and strange words. But that is exactly the problem—for both our culture and its religious traditions. Not being used to articulating such concerns, Australians can easily laugh off any attempt to express them. The extrovert, pragmatic quality of Australian culture has little patience with such non-evident dimensions of life. What is more, Australians are resolutely inarticulate about spiritual issues. The struggle and degradation of our past, to say nothing of the dust and distance and heat, somehow parched our spirits, and made us wary of anything seeming too lush and soulful. I think we can point to an even deeper reticence and reserve. It is as though anything truly significant, anything ultimately meaningful, cannot be a fitting matter for conversation. For us, the spiritual is not far from the obscene. Besides, if the sun is shining and the barbecue is sizzling, if the beer is cool and waves are thumping down there in the surf, moments of metaphysical reflection are necessarily rare!

Bruce Dawe seems to be getting at this strange reticence when he wrote of '...this southern church of silence/Where to speaks what's in the heart is some dishonour.'[15] The burden of finding words for 'what's in the heart' is a heavy one even for ministers of religion and religious educators in our country. Even the theologically adept, challenged by the realities of Australian culture, feel markedly tongue-tied. The general tone of our public discourse does not usually invite conversation about 'the deeper issues'. This, of course, has a lot to do with the lack of any assured place for religion in our public life. A US President can salt his discourses with quotations from the Bible. One does not expect such pieties from an Australian Prime Minister! Consequently, so much remains unsaid. Occasionally, it surfaces in a snarling confrontation of one kind or another. But for a politician, or, for that matter, anyone in public life, to appeal to deeper values is to risk a resentful rejoinder: 'Keep your values to yourself! This is no place for preaching!'

Yet these deeper values are approached as we try to talk about human rights in increasingly comprehensive and sophisticated ways: women's rights, ethnic rights, Aboriginal rights, gay rights, the rights of the handicapped, of the unborn, our common right to an ecologically sound environment. What passes unnoticed is that any appeal to human rights contains within it some sense of a universal order and human worth to which we are beholden. However unspoken, a reality is being imagined as involving human beings in a collaboration founded on something different from individual and group self-interest. It is at least the elemental stirrings of a larger integrity. But there the conversation seems to stop.

Recently a series of articles appeared as a booklet, *Australia Unveiled. The Changing Face of a Nation*.[16] It was produced by a combined *Age* and *Sydney Morning Herald* team, and was based on the latest census statistics. It presents itself as 'the most thorough portrait yet of Australia's reshaping forces—the style of the family; the astonishing tide of power to women;

the pampered generation that has the nation in its grip.'[17] Though it attempted to confine itself to statistics and anecdotal reportage, it could not conceal a sense of shock at the erosion of traditional values, and the extent to which Australia was changing. The 'pampered generation that has the nation in its grip', the 'baby-boomers' of the 1940s, come in for special treatment in an article entitled, 'Narcissism is booming':

> ...*the Me generation, born into unprecedented prosperity and cosseted in selfishness... They have been child-kings and child-queens, teenage idols of the marketers, participants in the sexual and social revolutions that have brought such vast change to Australia. And if they have a motto it would be: "ubi est meum?" (where's mine?).*[18]

While such statements are more or less a set piece in social comment regarding any Western society, the resentment felt against one generation conceals a problem that spans all the generations. After all, to the degree that such condemnations have a grain of truth, the 'Me generation' were crowned child-kings and child-queens by someone; someone 'cosseted them in selfishness'. The general values of the larger society are not mentioned. The 'Me Generation' did not drop out of the sky! Someone must have brought them into existence, educated them, shielded them from life's more self-transcending demands. It is a precious instance of our Australian style of knocking to scapegoat the post-War generation without a more general confession of sins—or aspirations, for that matter. More seriously, this 'unveiling of Australia' is typically Australian in its inarticulateness. The report is unable or unwilling to speak of values directly. Significantly, its moral content is left to the cartoonists (Spooner, Petty, Tandberg, Leunig, Moir).

As such a report stands, it is rather depressing: no indication of a deeper conscience is suggested, no one is cited as having a care for the country as a whole; no evidence of anyone feeling dissatisfaction at the oppressive materialism is brought forward; no mention is made of the vigorous protests of religious groups, artists or the ecologically-minded. All that is mute, or, more likely, left to find its own mode of communication. For 'the brave new ideas' in Melbourne are magnetic levitation, the O-Bahn, double-decker trains, people-planning, the ring road, dual occupancy, new-look housing, the very fast train, etc., etc.

The brave new world seems short on brave new values. On the other hand, in featuring questions relating to the choice of schools, above all, 'private schools', this report points to the fact that decisions are being made concerning the kind of values and orientation the rising generation should be given. A pithy statement in this context runs:

> *Education is a consumer item. It has become part of the general move toward consumerism and belief that you have to pay for anything that is worthwhile. Many believe that the more you pay, the more you get.* [19]

This is, of course, an extraordinarily despairing generalisation. Valuing a certain kind of education and being prepared to put your money where your heart is seems to be a long way from the crass materialism that this report implicitly laments. Admittedly, it *is* a source of concern for those who envision alternative education as a protest against the dominant, flatly secular and consumerist culture that their schools are becoming too much a resource for the economically privileged. But that matter is far more complicated, and the complication resides in the fact that there are values that money cannot buy; and that the greatest values are not notably rewarding in a financial sense. Since we shall be returning to the education issue, it is sufficient to note here that our unwillingness or inability to talk about these larger values makes education appear simply as a market commodity. If that is all it is, why should we bother? It would be merely a gigantic job-training scheme for a shaky Australia Inc.

To some of us it is an essential part of human integrity to educate children in our religious traditions; to others, as the frenzy of the D.O.G.S. case showed, such religious consciousness has no place in our culture. To Aboriginal Australians, particular places shine with sacred significance: the reality of the Dreaming. To others, there is no room for such ethereal apprehensions: the developer and the mining corporation know the really real. For many Australians, particular cultures and languages, histories and ways of life, are sacred, and judged essential to any worthwhile identity. To others, 'multiculturalism' is at best political cant, divisive of the 'real Australia'—which the 'real Australians' happen to run!

However improbable it might seem at first glance, human rights will eventually demand a new imagining. What is a right without an effort to imagine the worth of the suffering other? The language of responsibility is hardly possible without trying to imagine a more humane community. Concern for a common future carries within it a way of imagining the world otherwise.

Desert or Hidden Stream?

Somewhere, some original spiritual vision is still imagining a world of altruism and hope. Great spiritual traditions still nourish us in their hidden way. But, too often, spiritual depth, removed from any public conversation, is confused with the exotic or the faddish. The bored young 'leave the church', to whose radical imagination they were never introduced, only to apprentice themselves in the mystic lore of the East. Gurus proliferate, often with a capitalist eye on the 'stress management' market. One can understand a poet's question:

'Who shall wearily swim in this paddling pond of the Disneyland of the soul?'[20]

One of the fiercest poetic judgments made on our lack of spirituality is found in a poem by Jim McAuley. He likens the Australian soul to the landscape, so that both convey 'the faint sterility that disheartens and derides':

Where once was a sea is now a salty sunken desert,
A futile heart within a fair periphery;
The people are hard-eyed, kindly, with nothing inside them,
The men are independent but you could not call them free.[21]

For poets and artists—'the antennae of the race'—to express such judgments on the sterility and the futility, the emptiness and isolation of culture means that there is a resistant force at work. For such expressions to be published and read is an index of a current of protest against the psychological mutilation Australian culture tolerates. A cultural crown of thorns starfish can invade the living, shimmering reef of our consciousness. But for this hidden reef of spirit to appear so often in our poetry, in the novels (and other utterances) of Patrick White, in the stark forms of so much of our painting (Nolan, Pugh, Boyd,

Drysdale, Williams), in the evocative music of Sculthorpe and
Anthill, is indicative of this other current. It subverts the
superficiality of our unexamined 'way of life'.

In his well-known poem 'Australia', A.D.Hope catches the
sense of spiritual malaise :

Without songs, architecture, history:
the emotions and superstitions of younger lands,
her rivers of water drown among inland sands,
the river of her immense stupidity.

Floods her monotonous tribes from Cairns to Perth,
In them at last, the ultimate men arrive
Whose boast is not 'We live' but 'We survive',
A type who will inhabit the dying earth.

And her five cities, like five teeming sores,
Each drains her: a vast parasite robber-state
Where second-hand Europeans pullulate
Timidly on the edge of alien shores.[22]

The lack of deeper feeling, the sheer unawareness of a larger
vision, 'the immense stupidity', the monotony and timidity of
our aspirations, are here tellingly suggested in a way that
resonates with any aware Australian's experience. It is meant
to shock us into exploring larger versions of our existence. The
whole truth remains, typically, both inarticulate and repressed.

This cannot be the end of the matter. Is there a depth to our
characteristic silence in which something more deeply human
is hiding? To accept the above poetic judgments as the final
judgment would leave us in a state of pathological self-hatred.

Meaningful Silence

Hence, these soul-searchings have a positive aim. They are
meant to enhance and hone sensitivity to that deep level of
consciousness where integrity is formed, and a new imagining
begins. Neither silence nor inarticulateness necessarily mean
absence of spiritual depth. The lack of expression may be
merely an absence of the skill or opportunity to name what is
most meaningful; or, more simply, for whatever reason, having
no desire to do so. There are reasons in Australian history for
both these possibilities: our antipodean isolation, the brutality

13

of our historical origins   as a 'cesspool...the dregs of the
offscourings of all mankind' (Bishop Ullathorne), a general
sense of something new struggling for expression in the harsh,
raw world of Down Under. What Australians were about,
looked like 'no-thing' compared to older habits of thought and
expression. Australia had entéred into a kind of cultural 'cloud
of unknowing', its own *via negativa*, in which the lush
ideologies and cultured thinking of the old countries had to be
denied before the new reality could be expressed. Yet something was going on, even if it never reached full philosophical
expression or merited the attention of the theological traditions
available to us: we were involved in something, a new way of
being human, in the living and dying demanded in the condi-
tions of 'Down Under'.[23] Judith Wright catches the sense of the
original mystery of existence when she writes:

> *Living is dailiness, a simple bread*
> *that's worth the eating. But I have known a wine,*
> *a drunkenness that can't be spoken or sung*
> *without betraying it. Far past Yours or Mine,*
> *or even Ours, it has nothing at all to say;*
> *it slants a sudden laser through the common day.*[24]

Grace kept on being grace for us in the silences that inherently resist all expression.

This naturally touches on the religious question. A poet,
reviewing Les Murray's *Anthology of Australian Religious Verse*
suggests that 'wordless' character of mystery for which
Australians would seem to have a special affinity:

> *...just what is 'religion'? ...it comes as no surprise then, to find*
> *work by many of Australia's greatest writers here, many of whom*
> *would not call themselves religious, and who certainly would not*
> *call themselves Christian. But the book implies that the poet and*
> *the theologian can cover the same ground, they just approach it*
> *from different angles. I like this approach, as it forces truth to be*
> *separated from dogma and self-interest, it returns God to the*
> *wordless, and then tries to find words for him.*[25]

However much we might try to find words for this ineffable
mystery, it is no special service for Australians to attempt to
replace our silences with religious chatter. St Ignatius of An-
tioch wrote eighteen centuries ago, 'Those who hear the word

of God can also hear his silence.' The best words come from and return to silence. In the end, it is a matter of respecting both ends of the experience, even if our Australian experience makes us more familiar with hearing the silence rather than with speaking the word. To foreign observers it often appears that we have nothing important to say. There is something about us Australians that prefers to communicate in silences rather than in words. Perhaps we are defeated by it all, tongue-tied in the presence of ultimate things. Perhaps we feel safer with the great things left unsaid, meaning them only in silence: we, the inarticulate, offering our homage to the ineffable. Ultimate truths are not to be captured in any expression. They are not the exclusive possession of anyone; nor are they to be taken merely on anyone's authority. For someone to really know these things is to keep a decent reserve, to hold what is sacred in silence. I suppose it blends in with all the other silences about us—the haunting silence of the bush; the daunting silence of the desert; the surrounding silence of the sea; even the silence of our conversations when, as we talk of sport or work, or yarn over the fence in the front garden, we are quietly assessing whether someone is really a good bloke, or whether some woman is…well, what *do* we say when we admire women and never quite know how to express it?

For anyone to speak of these great matters is to appear oddly ridiculous. If you know, those who know you know, recognise your knowing silence.

> *Then, as the poets, who alone defend*
> *That darkness out of which our light is won,*
> *Strengthen my love—but flash no beam upon*
> *The future; show the meaning, not the end!*
>
> *Lest the mind, knowing too well the things to be,*
> *Lose its blind courage and forget its part,*
> *And no more trust its blind lightnings, nor the heart*
> *Kindle and quicken at the mystery.*[26]

There must be room for this kind of silence. It is a good irony to keep the contrast alive between verbal glibness and the reticence of deep communication. Such a sense of shared irony on all that is pompous, on all who are too full of their importance, is at the root of both the 'mateship' and the irreverence which were so much part of our, now mythic, past.

The Language of Soul

Still, some words, some effort of imagination, is necessary, not to replace the deep silence of life but to serve it. If we do not risk such words, silence can be misinterpreted. It drifts into a mere superficial tolerance that really feels nothing and has nothing to say. Without trying to find some words for the heart and its secret ironies on those who know too much, that very irony might easily become a sardonic, defensive isolation from the demands of larger imagining.

That is why this issue of 'spirituality' is a challenge. It is a weak word in a world of theories and science and technical know-how. Compared to the taut scientific language, or logical analysis and empirical experiment, it seems as ethereal as the mist around the mountains. It shrouds the reality that only the geologist can classify, the engineer control, the real estate developer make available for ownership. But really it stands for those neglected reaches of our humanity that cannot be quantified: an inwardness that superficiality often conceals or denies; a way of imagining a larger belonging to the community, to the world, to the ultimate reality. It is the domain of what tends to remain unspoken amidst our usual pre-occupations, habitual compromises and strident confrontations.

Les Murray, reflecting on his experience of compiling his anthology of Australian religious verse, makes a series of arresting observations:

> ...it was striking how much of the decent religious poetry in this country dated from the period since Word War II; this is where the preponderance lay, and I left readers to mull over possible reasons why. I hesitate to give my opinion even now, though it is hard to resist the speculation that a decline in religious certainty has provoked an upsurge in searching and questioning—and a decline in an odd sort of anti-religious hectoring, which required a firm opponent to batter against. Things have arguably gone too far for that now, and the near total divorce of State from any underlying religious ethic has produced not 'freedom' but a terrifying void against which comfortable old Enlightenment audacities are meaningless. It is generations since being an agnostic involved any daring, and atheism tends to put one into coercive rather than generous company. More seriously, whether we believe in the soul or not, neither of these positions feeds it; we feel its hunger as a matter of experience, and have nothing to feed on but our own

selves. *At bottom, we cannot build a satisfying vision of life upon agnostic or atheist foundations, because we can't get our dreams to believe in them.*[27]

The established agnosticism which marks most areas of public life here is facing its own kind of challenge. What Les Murray said of poetry, Rosemary Crumlin parallels in her comments on 'religious' art in Australia in her magnificent *Images of Religion in Australian Art*.[28] It seems that our culture is beginning to feel more of a need for the transcendent dimension of life. It is the horizon of a greater daring, in 'more generous, less coercive company', in resistance to the secularist establishment. In a time of massive disillusionment, we begin to hunger for the true centre of things, and begin to imagine the world otherwise.

In a recent high-level symposium on Australia as *Terra incognita*, the 'unknown land', the North American editor alludes to the unknown or at least unacknowledged presence of religion in our culture:

> To dwell on these points is to reflect also on who feels 'liberated' in Australian society today, how that 'liberation' defines and expresses itself. It is to ask about the constraints in Australian society, constraints which derive in part from the values of a people who are not given to speaking too abstractly, who are constantly charged with not encouraging the growth of the 'high timber' in their midst which so impresses outsiders. How are all these contradictions to be explained? While Australian's 'civil religion' is not a theme of this volume—it is perhaps an American concept, at least in its modern form—such religion exists in Australia, and Gallipoli is only one of its major twentieth-century totems. Patriotism in not unfashionable in Australia, not unknown. To understand the Australian preoccupation with success and heroism, failure and defeat, equality and independence, is to know why those who see the country's twentieth- century religion principally as a worship of the sun are using a simple journalistic formula in a semi-jocular fashion. The questions conveniently avoided by such levity are whether new 'religions' do exist, what they are, whether they are significant, what they reveal about contemporary Australian society.[29]

A Search for Wholeness

Who does feel really liberated among us? How does a new imagining arise against the spiritual oppressions of our present and our past? Such are the questions that are the concern of spirituality. It means to be a consistent protest against anything that would truncate our humanity, mutilate our sensitivities or stunt the creativity of imagination. In an older language, it protects and releases 'the soul', where this means the transcendent dimension of the self as it reaches deeper than the superficial obsessions of culture, and ranges broader than our society's routine preoccupations. Spirituality recognises that the 'self' is open to an infinity that cannot be boxed or packaged into a secure possession. In the oldest tradition of philosophy and mysticism, the soul can only be content with mystery: *anima est quoddamodo omnia* (the soul is open to all things). Such matters can only be spoken of in the larger, more evocative fashion which Murray has termed 'wholespeak':

> *I call properly integrated poetic discourse Wholespeak, while discourses based on the supposed primacy or indeed the exclusive primacy of daylight reason I call Narrowspeak. The former embraces all good poetry, including that of religion, the latter embraces most of the administrative discourse by which the world is ruled from day to day, as well as most criticism.* [30]

What we are attempting here is a form of such 'wholespeak' as we explore the ultimate dimensions of human existence and the manner in which they occur in Australian culture. The 'wholespeak' of soul and art come together in James McAuley's poem, 'Time out of mind'. Though it is one individual's poetic expression, it inspires a more general reflection on Australian history and culture:

> *In youth my range*
> *was fear, vanity, lust.*
> *Shall I take in exchange*
> *Fatigue, rage, self-distrust?*
>
> *Only those joys that lie*
> *closest to despair*
> *are mine to hold on by*
> *And keep me clear.*
>
> *Yet at best or at worst*
> *this unknown self will see*
> *What its Creator first*
> *thought it to be.*

But I shall know this
Only in knowing
My self's Self, who is, and is
The end of my going.[31]

The quest for the 'self's Self' is at once aided and distracted
by the ever-expanding world of objects of the information
explosion. Never before has the scientific mind been so inclined
to amazement at the complexity and extent of a dimly known
universe.[32]   Never before have so many dramatic responsibilities erupted into the human consciousness. Yet never
before have we suffered from so much 'narrowspeak'—knowing more and more about less and less. Human consciousness
is drenched with a flood of mass-produced images as modern
advertising seduces the mind from thought and pollutes the
symbols of the inner landscape of our feelings. To keep one's
bearings in such a world of wonder, responsibility, confusion
and breakdown means searching for a point of spiritual integration from which we might begin to imagine the world
more hopefully and anew.

Any such integration and imagination will have to bear in
mind the huge shifts of consciousness occurring in modern
history. Older patterns of self-awareness have exploded. For
example, in the West, the individual self has to contend with
the social self of solidarity as Marx propounded it in his
revolutionary awareness. It has to deal with the hidden self that
Freud uncovered, and with the archetypal self that Jung
discerned in the ruins of our technological civilisation. The East
too has problems on a similar scale. The millennial harmonious
self of classical Buddhist and Chinese thought had its brutal
challenge: for into its sense of social and cosmic harmony has
entered the Long March of the Maoist revolution. The other
classic experience of the self was that of Hinduism. Here the
concrete ego is merely an appearance, to be finally immersed
into the real self of the Brahman. This, too, is facing its crisis.
For it has to accommodate the demands of modern politics and
social responsibility. The Untouchables of modern India also
have a vote!

On this subject, there are, of course, libraries of literature
indicating the dimensions of the self. One would have to list
such key figures as Jung, Piaget, Erickson, Frankl, Lonergan
and Fingarette; such commentators as Kohlberg, Fowler,
Gould, Loevinger, Egan, Conn, Moore, Doran, Assagioli, and

on the Australian scene, Frank Fletcher, Ronald Conway, Mary Anne Confoy, with their different points of view. While it takes no great effort to document the contemporary concern for the forgotten self of our extrovert and technological era, it is not an easy matter to evoke the reality in the concrete. But there are certain positions on which philosophers, psychologists, educationalists and theologians tend to agree. Might I suggest four areas of convergence:

First, the human self is a given in the mystery of consciousness. It is not one object among many, but the 'I' and 'we', the subject who sees and hears, means and seeks all the variety of objects within the human horizon.

Second, it is a continuously unfolding self. The self is a 'self-in-process'. It is the consciousness which expands in the variety of its activities. Typically, it develops through many stages.

Third, it is a self that expands and develops through a radical self-transcendence. This is most experienced in what is usually called 'conscience'. It is the ongoing struggle to leave behind inauthentic versions of self. It aims at fuller self-realisation in a wider world of meaning, a more determined pursuit of truth, a deeper commitment to value, a more self-surrendering relationship to the mystery of it all.

Fourth, this unfolding self is earthed and embodied in a particular dramatic history and culture. The soul always has a body. Though each human being is a self, no one is a self 'in general', more or less haunting the world. We are selves earthed, embodied in this time, this place, this history, this culture, this whole social and physical environment. Hence the justification of turning our attention to the texture of the Australian experience of selfhood.

'The Burning Soul'

This sense of the mystery of the self is caught in A.D. Hope's 'Ode on the Death of Pius the Twelfth'. Here the poet finds himself pondering on the mysterious inwardness of life:

> *Seven years have passed, and still, at times, I ask*
> *Whether in man, as in those plants, may be*
> *A splendour, which his human virtues mask,*
> *Not given to us to see?*

He ponders on the emergence of another dimension of human consciousness—maturity, 'the ecstasy of fire', 'the burning soul', a tranquillity beyond the agitation of mere desire:

If to some lives at least there comes a stage,
When, all the active man now left behind,
They enter on the treasure of old age,
This autumn of the mind.

Then, while the heart stands still, beyond desire
The dying animal knows a strange serene:
Emerging in its ecstasy of fire
The burning soul is seen.

This spiritual dimension, achieved so notably in old age, is shrouded in the ambiguities of vulnerable, limited humanity. The real depths of the human can pass unnoticed:

Who sees it? Since old age appears to men
Senility, decrepitude, disease,
What Spirit walks amongst us, past our ken,
As we among these trees,

Whose unknown nature, blessed with keener sense,
Catches its breath in wonder at the sight
And feels its being flood with that immense
Epiphany of light?[33]

The poem ends with the question similar to the one we are asking here. For to explore spirituality is to grapple with this 'unknown nature', these intimations of 'a keener sense', of wordless 'wonder'—the whole horizon of life revealed in 'that immense epiphany of light'.

Such a noble expression of 'the burning soul' can inspire our own more pedestrian 'soul searchings'. We have located such a search as a legitimate and, indeed, necessary exploration. It is true, as we have had plenty of occasion to note, that Australian culture is not particularly hospitable to what we are about. The 'narrowspeak' of our age, perhaps even the ironic reserve we favour, make it a difficult task. Yet, at a time when Bicentenary Australia is in danger of losing its soul, it is also a good time to try to save that soul as best we can.

Unless we Australians become capable of a 'wholespeak' conversation, the potential richness we aspire to in what is termed a 'multicultural society' will be intractably ambiguous. If the dominant, established secular culture has no room for

21

the centrality of religion around which a number of our immigrant cultures are formed, how will various ethnic groups,
profoundly animated as they are by Moslem, Hindu, Buddhist,
Sikh and the variety of Christian traditions, ever truly belong
here? Will becoming Australian be too high a price to pay?
These older cultures know nothing of the cultural repression
of religion which is the style, if not the policy, of contemporary
Australia.   Of course, all this is proportionately true of
Aboriginal culture and its millennial religious traditions. Is it
is one thing to give government recognition to 'sacred sites'.
But it is something else to have a shareable sense of the 'sacred'
so as not to make such recognition merely a gesture of indul-
gent tolerance.

When there is no real acknowledgment of the sacred, the
transcendent, the religious, as a cohesive force of cultures, the
society that aspires to be 'multicultural' is moving into troubled
waters. Do those who promote such a national policy know
what is at stake? Is it all an act of cynical social management
of minority eccentricities? Do they see such cultures as purely
decorative, a nice exotic additive to the basic national diet? Are
they really prepared for the fundamental differences of
worldview that are now mixing and inevitably colliding? Do
they expect that such cultures will slowly renounce their fundamental seriousness in an all-tolerant banality. Genuine
pluralism has to know how to respect religion and religions if
multiculturalism is going to mean anything. Have we the
spiritual resources to do that? I suspect that will be the big
question for the decades ahead. Our prevailing 'narrowspeak'
will become increasingly puzzled and uncomprehending, perhaps even ultimately hostile to the reality of multiculturalism
if a larger sense of ultimate meaning and values does not
emerge.

Similarly, if education, and even religious education, is
reduced to a form of 'narrowspeak', it will be a mutilation of
the self rather than its expansion and liberation. Even religious
knowledge becomes at best a catalogue of questions asked and
answers given without any intimate relationship to what we
consciously are as human beings. An education unconcerned
with the larger questions of life—faith, spirituality, human
dignity, moral responsibility—can become a systematic oppression of the human spirit.

1. See my 'Theology in an Australian Context' in *Discovering...*, Peter Malone (ed.), St Paul Publications, Homebush, 1988, pp. 51–2.

2. The problem is well expressed in Gerard Windsor, 'Problems of being a citizen in an Unlikeable Nation', *Compass Theology Review* 23, Summer, 1988, pp. 9–14.

3. Nicholas Jose, 'Cultural Identity: I think I'm Something Else', in *Australia: Terra incognita? Daedalus* Winter 1985, pp. 311–342. Hereafter, I will refer to this valuable symposium simply as *Australia...*

4. Jose, p. 318.

5. Jose, p. 333.

6. Jose, p. 319.

7. For different ways of approaching the question, compare Frank Fletcher, 'The Gospel and Australian Culture', *Exploring...*, p. 72; and Veronica Brady, 'Patrick White's Australia', *Intruders in the Bush*, John Carroll (ed.) Oxford University Press, Melbourne, 1982, pp. 192–206. Hereafter, *Intruders...*

8. Richard Kearney, *The Wake of the Imagination. Ideas of Creativity in Western Culture*, Hutchinson, London, 1988, pp. 361–371. I am indebted to Kearney for the quotations in the above paragraph.

9. Kearney, p. 364.

10. Kearney, p. 365.

11. Kearney, p. 366.

12. Kearney, p. 367.

13. Peter Kearney's songs, especially his recent collection, *The Year of God's Favour?*, Crossover Music, Mittagong, 1988, are an excellent example of this kind of imagination.

14. Patrick White, 'A Sense of Integrity', *Arena* 84, 1988, p. 103.

15. From the poem 'At Mass', cited in Peter Kirkwood, 'Two Australian poets as theologians: Les Murray and Bruce Dawe', in *Discovering...*, p. 195.

16. *Australia Unveiled. The Changing Face of a Nation*, Peter Smark and Judith Whelan (eds.), Age Publications, Melbourne, April 1989.

17. Smark and Whelan, Preface.

18. Smark and Whelan, p. 33.

19. Smark and Whelan, p. 37.

20. Hal Colebatch, 'Watching Hare Krishna Cultists at the University of W.A., *Anthology...*, p. 83. Reprinted from *Outer Charting*, © Hal Colebatch, 1985, by permission of Angus & Robertson Publishers/Collins.

21. James McAuley, 'Envoi'. Reprinted from *Collected Poems 1936–70*, © Norma McAuley, 1971, by permission of Angus & Robertson Publishers/Collins.

22. *Anthology...*, p. 228. Reprinted from *Collected Poems 1930–70*, © A.D. Hope, 1966, 69, 72, by permission of Angus & Robertson Publishers/Collins.

23.   For an abundance of apt quotation and wise comment, see E. J. Cuskelly, 'The Australian Heart: living faith in Australia', in the symposium, *A New Heart for a New World*, St Paul Publications, Homebush, 1986, pp. 245–259.

24.   From 'Grace', *Anthology...*, p. 283. Reprinted from *Alive Poems 1971–72*, © Judith Wright, 1973, by permission of Angus & Robertson Publishers/Collins.

25.   John Foulcher quoted by Les Murray in *Embodiment and Incarnation: Notes on preparing an Anthology of Australian Religious Verse*, Aquinas Library, Brisbane, 1987, p. 12. Hereafter, I refer to this seminal essay as *Embodiment...*

26.   From A.D. Hope's 'Invocation'. Reprinted from *Collected Poems 1930–70*, © A.D. Hope, 1966, 69, 72, by permission of Angus & Robertson Publishers/ Collins.

27.   *Embodiment...*, pp. 9–10.

28.   Rosemary Crumlin, *Images of Religion in Australian Art*, Bay Books, Kensington, 1989, pp. 14–19.

29.   Stephen R. Graubard in 'Preface to the Issue', *Australia...*, pp. v–xii.

30.   *Embodiment...*, p. 18.

31.   *Anthology...*, p. 275. Reprinted from *Collected Poems 1936–70*, © Norma McAuley, 1971, by permission of Angus & Robertson Publishers/Collins.

32.   See John Honner's *The Description of Nature*, Clarendon Press, Oxford, 1987.

33.   *Anthology...*, p. 285. Reprinted from *Collected Poems 1930–70*, © A.D. Hope, 1966, 69, 72, by permission of Angus & Robertson Publishers/Collins.

Chapter 2:
Talking Points and
Embarrassed Silences

God reveals himself precisely where he seems to imaginations nurtured by the Enlightenment's notions of God to be absent, in the physical necessity which presses so urgently in the landscape and in the spiritual desert inhabited by so many Australians, victims of misfortune, of subjection to impersonal fate. [1]

How does a 'Wholespeak' conversation arise in Australia? Obviously, it could be in a moment of inspiration—poetic, mystical—something like that; a transformative moment. There is no way of knowing when such events might occur. We can, however, do something in preparation for them. This would be more a case of forming our imaginations and informing our consciences in what we can deliberately attend to. It is a matter of recognising that the 'spiritual' is already there in daily experience. It is a dimension present, often uncomfortably, in the business of life itself. The conduct of any life is always taking us to some kind of 'limits', to use a word of a common currency in philosophical and theological circles. [2] There are outer limits or frontiers *to* the ordinary routines and arrangements of our existence, and near limits or edges *of* the mystery of existence we share. Such primal limits are usually listed with reference to fundamental human experiences such as birth and death, love, suffering, guilt and despair, wonder and joy. Rosemary Dobson, expressing a woman's experience of giving birth, very tellingly expresses one such 'limit experience':

> *Three times to world's end I went,*
> *Three times returned as one who brings*
> *Tidings of light beyond the dark*
> *But voiceless stays, still marvelling.*
>
> *But still, as Lazarus who was born*
> *Again beyond the edge of death,*
> *I see the world half otherwise*
> *And tremble at its mysteries.*[3]

Such verses conveniently introduce a consideration of the special 'limits' involved in our Australian experience. These are points at which we are typically inarticulate ('voiceless'), yet know that we are on the edge of something more ('the world's end'). It is where imagination is released to wonder at a larger wholeness of life, and to appreciate the world in a different light ('half otherwise'), a world in which one can resonate with deeper mysteries ('tremble at its mysteries').

Questions heard at the limits: embarrassed silences

So, basically, what we are looking at here is the experience of the transcendent hidden in our ordinary experiences when we come to the point where language runs out. This occasions sudden embarrassment in the conversation when the realities of death, love, suffering, artistic inspiration or ultimate responsibility crop up. Such telling points invite us to a deeper silence, and a more inspired expression: words of faith or art or passion arise out of silence and return to it. These telling points are the occasions when we are often inarticulate, speechless, do not know what to say. Ordinary preoccupations can't abide such heavy matters. Perhaps, too, our routine gravity cannot tolerate such light-heartedness. The people who dwell at the limits are the bereaved, the lovers, the sufferers, the mystics, the artists and the real thinkers. Because they call us to a larger horizon of living and being together, such as these are uncomfortable presences.

One aspect of the role of religious educators is to be critics of the culture. For any culture can try to domesticate the transcendent. This typically results in idolatry. We absolutise what we have produced, politically, economically, nationally. The culture closes in on itself, and soon, as is the way with all idolatry, human sacrifices are demanded as the price of stability. The sense of limits, of proportion, of the open space of history and creativity is lost. Hence religious educators have a prophetic role. They have to work to keep the horizons open, by toppling the idols and driving out the demons. Educators must lead out to the limits, the edges, the true openness of life. Without such an effort, our compulsive materialism, the short-sighted pragmatism of our problem solving, the flat dullness of our public discussions, our physical separation from major world crises, our embarrassment about all things spiritual, will cramp or stifle the spirit.

Without a sense of such limits, we are left on a very isolated dune, unconscious of the oceans of reality lapping around. If we are to hear the Word, we are well advised to provoke the ultimate, the most radical questions: What is the meaning of all our meanings, the sufficient reason for all the reasons we give, the ultimate value of everything we consider worthwhile? How, ultimately, do we belong together? What in life and even beyond it, might we hope for?

Now such questions leave everyone feeling dreadfully incompetent and exposed. They usually lie hidden in earnest conversation on such subjects as educational policies, unemployment, the care of the aged, bioethics, the acceptance of refugees, the rights of the Aboriginals, the future of 'multiculturalism', the 'feminist movement'. A space for such questions is carved into our psyches in the shock or revulsion occasioned by violence, injustice and tragedy. Unless we let our real questions surface, our national morality is at best an oppressive tolerance trying to balance the untroubled conscience of the many with the pressure tactics of the monomaniac few.

Let me, then, suggest a few limits which take us to the edge, to the question, 'what is it all about?' Such a question takes us away from the overloaded world of mere information into the luminous awe-full space where imagination can breathe. Each limit provides an invitation to 'wholespeak' as opposed to the 'narrowspeak' of superficial analysis.

In the following, I have summarised eight such limits relevant to our Australian experience.[4] Each of them indicates a dreaded outer limit of our experience. Each can occur as an embarrassed silence in our communication. Above all, each in an invitation to 'see the world half otherwise'.

Isolation

In some profoundly human sense, to be Australian is to be uprooted from any nurturing tradition characteristic of the older cultures of other countries. One of the women travellers in Murray Bail's *Homesickness*[5] expresses her reflections as follows:

> *We come from a country...of nothing really, or at least of nothing substantial yet. We can appear quite heartless at times. I don't know why. We sometimes don't know any better...even before we travel, we're wandering in circles. There isn't much we understand. I should say, there isn't much we believe in. We have rather empty feelings. I think we even find love difficult. And when we travel we demand even the confusions to be simple. It's all confusing, isn't it?*

And it is. Here we are all 'displaced persons'. Left with an eerie spiritual nakedness, we are unable to explain how we belong down here, save in a purely adventitious sense: be it because of the convict system or the Irish famine, the Gold Rush, or the political or economic realities that have forced our forebears to leave the place of their birth, we know a lot about what Heidegger called *Geworfenheit*—that sense of radical 'thrownness' or better 'cast-offedness' which more ordinary philosophers term 'contingency'.[6] Does this explain our materialism? Is this the radical meaning of our irony in the face of all pomposity? Is this the origin of our strange resignation to fate? The important question is this: What are we being invited to through this history of being 'cast off', in this 'down under', assigned, in our national beginnings, to the underside of history, where the 'home country' is always 'over there'? Is it the beginnings of a compassion for all peoples of the under-side of history? We have a sense of ourselves as a 'continent' of isolated experience, yet always with a 'defenceless coastline'.

The Aboriginal Presence

The Aboriginal people are not just a 'problem' to the white Australians celebrating the Bicentenary of European 'possession' of this country. They stand at a special limit to our sense of humanity. Their continuing existence embodies in the Aust-ralian conscience a challenge to the brutal greed that all but destroyed them. They stand for a largely unknown, more mysterious dimension of history, as it precedes our bicentennial history by well over thirty thousand years. Questions arise: How do they invite us to a more spiritual culture truly at home in the ecology of this land? How does their experience of 'sacred sites' awaken us to a range of values rather different from the concerns of the beef industry, the woodchip industry, the mining corporation and the real estate developer? The 'breadth' of European experience is challenged by the 'length and depth' of another way of being in the world. For Christians, how does this Aboriginal inheritance become another 'Old Testament' to enliven our awareness of the Spirit of Christ?

Our 'Commonwealth'

Even though many Australians are struggling financially, our style of life is affluent. In terms of food and health care, the family cat or dog is better off than most individuals in India, Africa and the Philippines. It is inconceivable that an increasingly sterile, aging, and affluent Australia will be able to hoard so much of the world's resources in the Asia that is developing about us. Within Australia itself, young families are increasingly barred from the possibility of building or owning their own home. What decisions brought about this crisis in urban real estate? Who made them? What values are at stake? What is going on when a government accepts an annual bill amounting to two billion dollars to cope with family breakup, yet allots less than $150,000 to marriage preparation? When nearly two million people in Australia live in comparative poverty, what are the responsibilities of the 5 per cent of Australians who own 45 per cent of the national wealth? Or of the 10 per cent who own 50 per cent? Of the 50 per cent who own 92 per cent? Of the bottom 50 per cent who have to make do with only 8 per cent? What judgment is being passed on us? What future would we welcome? If our hopes float with the dollar, if such hopes are buoyed up only by the gross mendacities of election promises; if the growing numbers of the truly rich are haunted by the terror of tax reform, one must ask in what sense would we welcome a true 'commonwealth' based on a more equitable sharing of goods?

Migrants

In the company of the great number of our fellow Australians who have migrated here from countries of older cultures, we touch on another kind of limit. They have come here looking for new hope in this country, be they British or Irish, Greeks or Italians, Vietnamese or Turks, Yugoslavs or Chinese. Can this be the place where people are redeemed from the destructiveness of particular pasts? Can we keep the creative elements of our particular histories? How is a new hopeful humanity possible in this Australian context? What new questions now arise out of our experience of radically different cultures amongst us—Muslim, Hindu, Sikh, Buddhist? How is our vision of the future hospitable to such histories of hope and suffering, and to so much expectation that Australia will be a 'promised land'?[7]

Leisure

Again this is a type of limit. If 'leisure is the basis of culture' (Josef Pieper), what might it do for us, to have the possibility of exploring and enjoying our environment more and more, be it on the beach, in the bush, in the rain forest, in the desert, and to become familiar with a 'nature' of marvellous variety? In our sport and recreation we enjoy breaking out of the routine structures of our workaday world. But into what? Into a more genuine enjoyment of life? Into a more celebratory way of being for body, spirit and community? Can we as individuals and groups still play, and prize our 'amateur status' in the sports we love, or have we lost the healthy human scale of our playing by projecting our playfulness onto media-packaged professionals of 'the entertainment and sport industries'?[8]

Sexuality

This is a limit-experience of a different kind again. It is often repressed by the brutalising stereotypes of 'Sheilas' and 'Ockers' and their modern equivalents. Niall Brennan's description of the Ocker is suggestive:

...that ignorant, loud-mouthed, bigoted, boozy bonehead with whom we are all too familiar...the type who, unable to speak his own language with any precision, is quick to trumpet his abuse at another for speaking another language; the type who is likely to be a chauvinistic pig, the type who is the worst possible advertisement for the country others have chosen to make their own.[9]

What is the meaning of the feminine in our self-consciously masculine tradition? What is the female equivalent of 'a good bloke' or a 'real mate'? How can we come to a new ability to accept the full mystery of our humanity in the exchanges of male and female? 'She'll be right'—but will she? Is there room for a new generativity and relationality? Is 'homosexual liberation' a complete cultural perversion, or is it struggling to allow for warmer relationships between men?[10]

Jill Conway, reflecting on 'Gender in Australia',[11] suggests the broader context of such questions:

Today the middle class has grown from the early colonial 10 per cent to 46 per cent of the population. But we have the evidence of a great literature and a great tradition in painting to suggest that they live in a bleaker emotional environment than history has given other bourgeois societies, and this affects the relationships of love and work that make up adult life in our times. Many Australian historians will disagree with such a view, but the history of the affective life of Australians is still to be written. We cannot yet know whether the current climate of political change will be an enduring one, one of those marking points in which a people set out in search of new meanings. To those who have lived these recent decades in Australia, the change seems momentous...

The Land

Our experience of the land inspires still other limits as most of us huddle around the seaboard. Dare we expose ourselves to the vastness, the silence, even the menace of this land? The land stands there, in the extent of its coasts and in its interior, as a symbol of the journey that all Australians must make: 'around Australia' to have some sense of the continent of our experience; 'to the interior', to the centre, away from the noise and business of the periphery, to the silence and dispossession of the desert. How can we come to dwell in the land in a way to nourish our souls? Once more, Nicholas Jose makes a pertinent remark:

For many people, the intractability of this antipodean land, and the strangeness of Australia's form of civilisation within it, has crystallised into a feeling that the land does not belong to Europeans in the way that it belongs to someone else: the Aborigines. Over and above the legal and political question of land rights for Aboriginals and the other attempts to compensate the atrocities of the past, the issue has unsettled some of the basic claims of Australian society, such as every man's right to prosper freely on land he has won for himself. The world that had grown up through free enterprising exploitation is at the cost of other worlds. A groping awareness of the Aboriginal presence, as purposefully nomadic, acculturated husbanders of the land for centuries, leads indirectly to a questioning of the fitness and necessity of the kind of society that Europeans have put in place of what was. The chastening realisation that there existed a quite different way of living with the land also opens up the possibility of alternatives that the present-day Australians may discover again.[12]

The Bicentenary

Recent celebrations pose their own kind of questions. Has our history ended in corruption and greed, and the celebration of what is most banal about us? So much has emerged as an 'ugly Australia' to be repudiated rather than to be celebrated. While we grant that the 'Bi' allowed for a certain amount of self-promotion on the part of politicians and media personalities, what significance did it really have for the rest of us? What were we celebrating? Why did the Aboriginals not take part? Why was the voice of the truly ethnic Australia hardly heard? Still no renaming of states, or cities or towns, still no flag of our own, still the representatives of the same old establishment celebrating the myths of the ways things were... Is there room for anything new? Is Patrick White's denunciation really too strong?

A large proportion of grown Australians remain children at heart— I see them as kidults. That's why they're so easily deceived by politicians, developers, organisers of festivals, and that is why they fail to dig the real purpose of a giant circus like the Bi.[13]

The more our Australian consciousness expand to such limits, the more a new imagining of what we are may emerge. For these limits, and many others that could be added,[14] are the real talking points: limits *to* narrowness, superficiality, pragmatism, ugliness; limits *of* a larger mystery of life, belonging, and identity... They mark the point at which being Australian needs to be re-imagined.

By facing such questions, by letting such 'limit-experiences' surface, a larger, transcendent dimension of selfhood comes to awareness. It is a self under the necessity of imagining a larger belonging. It is a soul that feels the restrictions of our cultural fixations. It is a heart feeling for something more than 'consumer satisfaction'. It is a spirit able to give thanks for the grace of life as it is being given to us in this place and this time, in this midst of this people.

Such questions, taken to their limits, are apt to disclose a 'depth dimension' in our culture, even if it is only a mysterious 'evanescent sense of questioning'. Such was one poet's prayer:

> *Incarnate Word, in whom all nature lives,*
> *Cast flame upon the earth: raise up contemplatives*
> *Among us, men who walk within the fire*
> *Of ceaseless prayer, impetuous desire.*
> *Set pools of silence in this thirsty land:*
> *Distracted men that sow their hopes in sand*
> *Will sometimes feel an evanescent sense*
> *Of questioning, they do not know from whence.*

What looks often to be a simple inarticulateness can be the appearance of 'pools of silence in this thirsty land'. There is an easily recognisable aspect of our culture; in its superficiality it may lead us 'to sow [our] hopes in sand'. Still, an intimation of another dimension keeps recurring:

> *Yet somehow between prayer and common sense,*
> *hearts may be touched, and lives have influence.*
> *And when the heart is once disposed to see,*
> *Then reason can unlock faith's treasury.*
> *To rapt astonishment is then displayed*
> *A cosmic map Mercator never made.*[15]

Once this other dimension is touched, traditions of faith can be re-appropriated with new moral and poetic imagination. The energies of wonder and compassion are released. 'Rapt astonishment' discerns, beyond the primitive, one-dimensional attempt of the old map-maker, the reality which is here, yet to be discovered.

1.   Veronica Brady, *A Crucible of Prophets. Australians and the Question of God*, Theological Explorations, Sydney, 1981, pp. 82–3. Reprinted by permission of the publisher.

2.   For a detailed treatment, see David Tracy's, *Blessed Rage for Order*, Seabury, New York, 1975, pp. 91–118.

3.   Rosemary Dobson, 'The Edge', *Anthology...*, p. 157. Reprinted from *Selected Poems*, © Rosemary Dobson, 1980, by permission of Angus & Robertson Publishers/Collins.

4.   For a related treatment, see Peter Kirkwood, 'Two Australian Poets as Theologians', *Discovering...*, pp. 195–216.

5.   Murray Bail, *Homesickness*, Penguin, Melbourne, 1980, p. 201.

6.   I owe this philosophical example to Dr Richard Campbell of the ANU, in a paper he read at an *ANZTS* Conference some years ago.

7.   Jim Houston, 'Australian Faces. Christians in a Multicultural Australia', *From Here to Where. Australian Christians owning the past—embracing the future*, Andrew Dutney (ed.), Uniting Church Press, Melbourne, 1988, pp. 65–78; Denis Edwards, 'Reflections on Multicultural Australia', *Compass Theology Review* 23, Summer 1988, pp. 1–8. For the reflections of an eminent Australian biblical scholar, Frank Moloney, 'A Theology of Multiculturalism', *Discovering...*, pp. 133–146.

8.   For a philosophical treatment of these issues, see Josef Pieper, *Leisure, the Basis of Culture*, Random House, New York, 1963; Thomas Ryan, *Wellness, Spirituality and Sports*, Paulist Press, New York, 1988. The broader context is well presented by Michael Casey in his article, 'Adding Depth to our Response to Local Culture', *Discovering...*, pp. 121–130.

9.   *Advocate*, March 3, 1983, p. 6.

10.   For a stimulating treatment of such issues, see Ronald Conway, *The End of Stupor? Australia towards the Third Millennium*, Sun Books, Melbourne, 1984, Chapters 3 and 4; John Smith, *Advance Australia Where?*, Anzea, Homebush, 1988, Chapters 6 and 7; George M. Crombie, 'The Divided Self: a Theological Reflection on "Mateship" in Australian Culture', *Australian and New Zealand Religious History*, R. Withycombe (ed.) ANZSTS/ATS, Canberra, 1988, pp. 194–207. Hereafter *ANZ Religious History...*

11.   Jill Conway, 'Gender in Australia', *Australia...*, p. 366.

12.   Nicholas Jose, 'Cultural Identity...', *Australia...*, pp. 337–338.

13.   'A Sense of Integrity', *Arena* 84, 1988, p. 98. For a more comprehensive view, see Graeme Ferguson, 'Echidnas and Myall Creek. Celebration and Suffering in 1988', *From Here to Where. Australian Christians owning the past—embracing the future*, Andrew Dutney (ed.), Uniting Church Press, Melbourne, 1988, pp. 45–61.

14.   Further material for such 'limit-experiences' abounds in Tom Inglis Moore's *Social Patterns in Australian Literature*, Angus and Robertson, Sydney, 1971.

15.   James McAuley, 'A Letter to John Dryden', *Anthology...*, p. 173. Reprinted from *Collected Poems 1936–70*, © Norma McAuley, 1971, by permission of Angus & Robertson Publishers/Collins.

Chapter 3:
Having a Heart: with
whom do we stand?

The ways we look after one another catch the eye in the Honours Lists and the latest Australia Day was celebrated with 40 categories worthy of distinction. In the highest degree was the Chairman of World Expo 88.

I was catching up with the press coverage of all this while the Prime Minister's message was broadcast on the radio. He was talking about the binding of Australians together, 'whatever their origins, a common commitment to Australia and Australian values'. This List of Honours illustrated the values he must have been speaking of right then, if his words were to mean anything. We had honoured, that very day, 56 compatriots for business and professional expertise. The next highest value was sport—no surprise here—but it led by six place-getters, on my count, ahead of work done in migrant communities, work described in the phrase 'whatever their origins'. Anyone tipped for commendation who worked for Aboriginal Australians was on especially long odds. I could find only seven. Religions earned one more.

These cannot be the values the Prime Minister was at that moment calling 'a fair go for all, tolerance and insistence on the rights of others'. It seemed to me there was no cynicism in his voice. It felt more like a rising nostalgia but a nostalgia for the future, the loss to him of the once possible. [1]

A fundamental expansion of soul is the pursuit of values. This is the specifically moral consciousness, or 'conscience' as it is generally called. Far from implying an individualistic soul-culture, it is about the way we imagine our most radical belonging to others, and the manner we establish contact, in heart and eye, with those who suffer. 'Behind and beyond the image a face resides: the face of the other will never let the imagination be.'[2]

Ethical Imagination

Such ethical imagination takes us out of the isolated self and its gratification, into the common good, the world of collaboration in social reality. It is not simply a matter of contemplating our world in a new way but a way of actively imagining it otherwise. Conscience, and the images and the values which nourish it, keeps facing us with the questions of what we want to make of ourselves, what we are doing with our freedom, how we are contributing to the humanisation of the world.

The ethical imagination projects us into the area of uncomfortable solidarity with others. It is that centre within ourselves at which we stop being cosmic drifters and social conformists, and begin to resist, in the name of something more, something other.

The moral imagination is the basis of the age-old philosophies of a cosmic moral order or a universal 'natural law'. Such perennial wisdom has found new support as thinkers probe the foundation of human rights, promote the just sharing of the world's goods, raise anew the issue of a total abolition of war and, of course, give themselves to the great ecological concerns of our day. On the other hand, because it is a human imagining, it has to allow for all the dramatic untidiness of the human condition. Since we belong together as a community of free human agents, personal conscience has to be respected. Persuasion, the contagion of moral authority, not coercion, is the only way values are communicated.

There is the paradox: the human values that enable any commonwealth to exist, make for a wholeness that must allow for individual freedoms. Without the wholeness, no society can be sustained; without the individual freedom, no society is worth maintaining.

Our Permanent Poem

Les Murray imagines our ethical connectedness in a refreshing-ly original way. He likens it to a kind of permanent inner poem we carry within. It is a tacit but authoritative expression of what we know we are called to be. It is the point where we cannot lie to ourselves, where the untruths, deceptions, all the uncriti-cal myths that conveniently nourish our self-deceptions, are sensed for what they are:

> *If there is anywhere within us a sort of embassy of such wholeness, it may be what we call our conscience—which some at times to avoid the Christian theology of it, prefer to call their integrity. In my experience, conscience shares with art an ability to be instan-taneously and convincingly there and a total resistance to untruth (you can't lie in art, any more than in prayers) and it has an eloquence both in and beyond our words, and a stern logic that operates without any need of them... In some ways, I would go close to saying that the conscience resembles a permanent poem of ourselves which we carry within ourselves, though not one which claims our attention unless we try to circumvent it, or some external influence challenges it.* [3]

To reflect on Australian spirituality as an ethical imagination means attempting to elucidate this permanent inner poem of our national selfhood. Somehow it is there to be appealed to. Somehow it is oddly resistant to other pressures. Yet, compared with blaring, sensate, self-serving certainties which pervade what often passes for Australian culture, it is a comparatively inarticulate voice. No doubt, the North American sociologist, Robert Bellah, was getting at the same thing in his aphorism, 'No one has changed a great nation without appealing to its soul.' [4]

A remarkable effort in imagining this 'permanent poem' of Australian conscience is Manning Clark's six volume *History of Australia*. [5] It is a sustained effort to put Australia in touch with its conscience. His prophetic judgment upon the utilitarianism and brutality of our history is an attempt to redeem from our past a 'heroic witness to a larger spirit'. His concern is always to place Australia's history in the matrix of the great human questions. His categories are not purely empirical—the in-dividual and the state, for example. He allows for a larger more imaginative and humanly sensitive interpretation of our history. That is why his judgments can be so searching. He is trying to see things, as he has often expressed it, *sub specie aeternitatis*—in terms of the ultimate worth of Australian history.[6]

Conscience, and its compassionate imagination, despite the tender meaning of such terms, faces us with hard questions: What kind of Australia do we want to be? What kind of multi-cultural openness to immigrant and refugee should we practice? How should our national budget be apportioned? What is our response to the massive past injustices inflicted on the Aboriginal inhabitants of this *Terra Nullius*? Why care for the poor, the elderly, the unborn, the future generations? How can a government subsidise a national meeting of 'the sex industry' and be so inarticulate about the integrity of the family? What is going on when a government accepts a huge annual bill to facilitate the breakup of marriages and families and contributes so little to marriage preparation.[7] Why should rain forests not be logged? What are the responsibilities of the one per cent of Australia's population who control 20-25 per cent of its private wealth?[8] Of the 5 per cent who own 45 per cent of the national wealth? How do we ultimately belong together as one people? How should we? With whom do we stand, and against what? For whom do we speak?[9]

The Passing of Innocence

In so many ways the old innocence has gone the way of the old egalitarianism.[10] The dramatic increase in wages has accompanied endemic unemployment. Those who have provoked the phrases, 'the Revolt of the Rich' and 'the New Greed', are remarkably evasive when it comes to paying taxes. And, as unionists continually remind us, 'fat cat' public servants preside over an economy in crisis. More darkly, dramatic evidence of corruption at a high level in the judiciary, law-enforcement agencies, and even government, have taxed the resources of a series of Royal Commissions. Then, there is a crisis in all the professions who have been prepared to trade their rather exalted status in Australian society for material gain. And the media—owned by whom?—increasingly show millionaires at work and play. Hugh Stretton, in a fine article terminating with 'gloomy conclusions', writes:

For a decade or so now, many of the rich of the Western world have been attacking its poor, increasing its inequalities, and denigrating its more compassionate ideas and institutions with renewed vigour and self-righteousness. In the lurch to the Right, the tax revolt, the use of deliberate unemployment as a macroeconomic device, the voguish cult of self and selfishness, and other manifestations of the New Greed, plenty of Australians have joined in with a will. It was not surprising that the traditional rapacious rich should do so. What is frightening for the future is that they seem at times to be getting a popular majority for it. [11]

As Stretton goes on to remark, there is really very little criticism of the New Greed by intellectuals and social scientists. The critics tend to be uninfluential: 'Women, social workers, Marxists, a few radical sociologists and political scientists'. [12] It is hardly surprising that the Catholic bishops have initiated a widespread consultation on the just distribution of wealth in Australia. Nor was the resultant obloquy unexpected. [13]

Another commentator remarks that the growing stridency of Australian self-assertion since the early seventies has concealed many uncertainties. Neither he nor I can resist quoting from Patrick White again: [14]

As Patrick White recently remarked, 'We have been served up a lot of claptrap about the need for national identity. We have been urged to sing imbecile jingles, flex our muscles like the sportsmen from telly commercials, and display a hearty optimism totally unconvincing because so superficial and unnatural.'

In its image-making for both national and international consumption, Australia appears to have been remarkably successful. However, the fabrication of self-inflated images has confused the deeper issue. The genuine 'Australia' is not there simply to be to be proclaimed or packaged as an image for the tourist industry. It still has to be formed.

Owning the Past

How then is the genuine Australia to be formed? A true part of the Australian poem is its original political originality. Overseas a secret ballot is often known as an 'Australian ballot'. In those former times of the gold and wool boom our democratic forms were the envy of the world. But the perverse side: our society was closed to all save white settlers. Today our frontiers exclude no one on the basis of race or colour, and that brings with it new issues of national integrity, the dread point for some, when the old white Australia has to die into something new—multi-racial, multi-cultural, Eurasian, Asian... How will the old poem be re-expressed in this new context?

Though a good number of Australians welcome the new mix of peoples, not many ask whether there is much real 'mixing' going on. Violent instances of racism, noted even by the captain of the West Indian cricket team in a recent tour, makes us wonder whether Australia is on the way to becoming a society of largely separated ethnic and racial enclaves. This, in turn, raises more fundamental questions: To whom does Australia choose to relate to in the world today? How do we define such relations? How do we envision our future in Asia and in the Pacific in the next millennium?[15]

Such issues are not going to be resolved without some deep searching of the heart. If we are to confront the threat and promise of our future, we must expect dread, hope, risk, and anger to become familiar, if uncomfortable, feelings.

Again part of the poem is our national sympathy for the underdog. Such a sympathy expects that decent public provision will be made for individuals in distress. But even such a sturdy value has to be 'transvalued' now that its compromises and selectivity is more clearly seen. For in many ways this sympathy was 'a conformist compassion'.[16] As the history of our treatment of Aborigines, the Irish and the Chinese shows, it was notably intolerant of minorities. It was the compassion of the closed shop. Basically, such a compassion was a utilitarian commitment rather than genuine solidarity with the oppressed and the sufferer. Looking after one's own often masked brutal exclusion.

A Commonwealth of Values

If such a conformist kind of compassion is really the half-hearted moral reflex of those jealous of their own position, it is now under pressure to expand into a more genuine integrity. What most challenges our prevalent utilitarian tradition is the question of human rights. In the last two decades, a variety of such challenges have been issued to the established ideology.

The most significant clashes have been between Aboriginal rights and the ideology of white settlers; between women's rights and the exclusive myths of mateship; between conscientious objection and the solidarity of the 'diggers'. Then migration and more flexible work structures have challenged the unreflecting solidarity of the trade unions. More subtly, the claims of the environment have been urged against the established right to own and exploit the land.

When such issues are discussed, the problem is to find both a language and a forum in which to articulate this new comprehension.[17] To some degree, the utilitarian tradition can cope by striking an appropriate bargain with a powerful lobby. But deeper issues such as the reality of the rights concerned, compensation for past denial of such rights, the occurrence of new values, leave our social institutions notably tongue-tied. Our ethical imagination evidences an odd exhaustion when human rights and environmental activists often have to call upon outside support to advance their case, be it from the United Nations, the World Council of Churches, a visiting pope, the International Women's Movement, the World Heritage Organisation, international legal conventions, or whatever.

Failures in Imagination

Take, for example, the Australian style of debates on abortion, in-vitro fertilisation, the rights of the family, Asian migration. The day tends to be carried by the pressure group. There is no conspiracy of imagination. Such issues, because they usually have the makings of a good story, are, eventually, picked up by the media, the mirror image of our conformist compassion. Quickly the issues congeal into images suggestive of a generalised and undiscriminating social feeling. The critical issue of Asian migration can be lost by the featuring of the crimes of Vietnamese youth gangs, or the impending threat of Chinese triads from Hong Kong, in reports about dissatisfied Japanese tourists, or in headlining the extent of Japanese investment in local real estate. Similarly, smiling parents rejoicing over the birth of their IVF success can conceal our absence of any moral or legal grasp of such momentous scientific intervention in human reproduction.[18] An image of a youth sleeping on the street can well suggest the plight of 'fifty

41

thousand homeless children', but stops deeper discussion on our lack of care for the homes, the families, and even the marriages involved in such a disaster. Arresting media images do not exhaust the capacities of moral imagination—especially when they typically lead to a demand for more government funding!

Political Imagination

Little wonder in a world of such complexity that 'some issues are organised into politics while others are organised out'(Schattschneider). For the growing number of issues that are organised 'in', parliamentary debate restricted to adversarial warfare is of the crassest kind'.[19] Getting the numbers to make one more law seems to be the only answer. Compulsive legalism tries to plug one more gap. The larger imagining is deferred. Then there are the issues that are organised 'out': the Asianisation of Australia, the rights of the family, a genuine reconciliation with the Aboriginal people. A confused sense of repressed concern helps no one. Democracy as, first of all, a way of imagining the life of human beings together, is jeopardised. Such imagining is never merely bipartisan agreement; nor, for that matter, a sweetheart deal between the parties not to raise some issues. The authentic human voice, speaking out of moral imagination, has usually been heard only from smaller parties, independents not tied to the party platform, and semi-political associations concerned with peace, social justice, ecology, cultural minorities, family life and so forth. Perhaps the recently launched Rainbow Alliance will dramatise the extremely restricted nature of our political conversation. Perhaps it will succeed where others have failed, by being, not merely an imaginatively-named organisation, but a forum and a force for a new imagining in Australian life. Whatever the case, one wonders if the influence of the church should be more concerned to inspire the larger imagination and the conversation that flows from it, rather than allowing itself to be reduced to one more self-interested lobby. The church is still the only institution in Australian society equipped to initiate a conversation on the moral order.[20] In a significant book treating of the Catholic church's relationship to North American society and culture,[21] a North American Lutheran, Richard J. Neuhaus, has made what, to many, would appear a surprising point. He argues that Catholics should assume their rightful place in the task of forming a culture and, indeed, shaping a philosophy in and for a pluralistic and democratic society, and in 'constructing a religiously informed public philosophy for the American experiment in ordered liberty'.[22] Apparently fellow Christians expect more of the Catholic tradition than Catholics do themselves! Perhaps perversely, Australian society expects a lot more of the church, however sceptical we may be as a people on the subject of religious authority. It is not hard to get politicians to speak at church-sponsored meetings on moral issues! I make this observation with the understanding that the moral order is a radical imagining of our human community. Without that kind of belonging any society is impossible. It is inherently inclusive: without it we collapse into our own chaos of our private egoisms. The following words were not written with Australia in mind; but they are worth reading in the light of our present problems:

> *Egoism is in conflict with the good of order. Up to a point, it can be countered by law, the police, the judiciary, the prisons. But there is a limit to the proportion of the population that can be kept in prison and, when egoism passes that limit, the agents of the law and ultimately the law itself have to become tolerant and more indulgent. So the good of order deteriorates. Not only is it less efficient but also there is the difficulty of exercising even-handed justice in deciding which injustices are to be winked at. The practical expression is apt to be whose social sins are to be forgiven, and whose are to be punished, and then the law is compromised. It is no longer coincident with justice. In all likelihood it becomes to a greater or lesser extent the instrument of class.*[23]

Traditional Values

This is not to say that there is a lack of moral values prized in this country. Our history has demanded of us a rugged appreciation of our fellow battlers. 'Loyalty to one's mates' is something of a primary value. The symbols of Gallipoli and life in the bush attest to this.[24] The issue is how such moral images can be re-imagined in the interests of a more inclusive solidarity with those most struggling in our midst. If this is not attempted, then such prize loyalties degenerate into what

one can 'do for my little mate' (to use the phrase made
notorious in one of our legal scandals). When the foundations
of our loyalties and commitments remain unexplored an increasingly chaotic pluralism results. Or if it is left more or less
to good instincts formed in particular historical conflicts such
as wartime experience, trade union solidarity, in a variety of
activist concerns on particular moral issues (such as peace,
religious freedom, women's liberation, the rights of the unborn, ecological issues, Aboriginal rights) any moral conversation is at best a rapidly sloganised, single-issue cacophony. To
cite Lonergan again:

> While the individual egoist has to put up with the public censure
> of his ways, group egoism not merely directs development to its own
> aggrandisement but also provides a market for opinions, doctrines,
> theories that will justify its ways and, at the same time, reveal the
> misfortunes of other groups to be due to their depravity. Of course
> as long as the successful group continues to succeed, as long as it
> meets each new challenge with a creative response, it feels itself the
> child of destiny and it provokes more admiration and emulation
> than resentment or opposition. But development guided by group
> egoism is bound to be one-sided. It divides the body social not merely
> into those who have and those who have not but also make the
> former the representatives of the cultural flower of the age to leave
> the latter apparent survivals from a forgotten era...[25]

Breakdown in the Conversation

If they lack the larger, more compassionate imagining we have
been referring to, the selective moralities of the single issue are
enclosed in self-righteousness. The result is limitless instances
of confrontation with the larger community to the detriment
of any sense of radical common good. To be disappointed in
such confrontation induces a gnostic or perhaps Mafia-like
ethic likely to resist an open social conversation. If it is successful, it is the success of the pressure group which bends the law
to its interest. The 'wowser syndrome' prevails. It is willing to
impose its commitments on others by rejecting the more
general, complex testimony of human experience. The moral
becomes identified with the legally attainable; and the legal is
the imposition of those who have grabbed power first. It has
no confidence in a commonwealth imagined through moral

conversation. For in such a commonwealth, the leading notion is the responsibility of society as a whole, the main agent is the responsible citizen. This is far removed from a consumerist version of society in which each one is a relatively alienated individual demanding an ever increasing list of often newly discovered 'rights'. There are limits to what is possible when social communication is restricted to the chant of the 'demo': 'What do we want?' 'X'! When do we want it? 'Now!'

Philosophers have long been pointing to the breakdown in moral discourse.[26] The poll is increasingly the measure of public morality. When there is no shared vision, no shared sense of humanity, no common story orienting the direction of our history, morality has to become either a matter of isolated personal taste, or a matter of political expediency. The only acceptable evidence is based on the pollsters' researches, where what is most self-transcendent in human beings is counted alongside with what is most self-destructive. Morality is simply social quantity. We cannot blame politicians for auctioning their policies. They have to live and work with a dismal diagnosis of the society they serve: the 'body politic' twitches only in its economic nerve.

Our Habits of the Heart

A team of alert US analysts of society and culture, led by Robert Bellah, reflected recently on the North American white experience in their *Habits of the Heart. Individualism and Commitment in American Life.*[27] They pointed to the fragmenting of the US experience into a private individualism. The national cohesion built on social responsibility had collapsed. In a way that would dismay Australians, they called for the development of new consciousness, 'new habits of the heart', in which the great American dream of a new, free socially-responsible nation could still be a significant historical commitment. The two most fruitful sources for this they found to be the Judaeo-Christian biblical tradition and the enlightened republican vision of their founding fathers. Both these resources are still part of the cultural psyche of North Americans, however buried or inhibited they may have become.

North American analysis such as this provokes similar questions for us—even if we know that we have no similar answers, at least not to the public extent that they are available to 'religious USA'. What is the fundamental and enduring vision of ourselves as a nation? We cannot so readily appeal to a shared biblical faith: the religion of 'God's policemen' not to mention 'the flogging parsons' or the subversive Catholicism of the dissident Irish, made religion a dubious entity for us in the public domain. The wowser and the bigot have done their damage. As for our founding fathers: on this 'fatal shore', they perpetrated and perpetuated a monstrosity of such depravity that only our isolation from the civilised world saved it from a more prompt condemnation. On both these issues we have to be beware of our past.

Exhausted Imagination?

The flagship of Catholic commitment to Australian culture has been the enormous institution of church schools. As the oppressed Irish have now moved up the economic and social ladder, this institution has become one huge question. Has the sense of dramatic struggle for legitimate freedoms dwindled into a conformist caution—even away from authentic moral consciousness still flickeringly alive in our society? Has this striking success story ended in a relaxed, government-funded celebration of having made it in the WASP world? Have the original energies of such imagination become mere respectability? The church's involvement in education is making it once more ask how it might provide a schooling of the heart in the larger process of contributing to the formation of a more compassionate society. When the young are exposed to the deadly realities of teen suicide, sexual exploitation, drug abuse, the collapse of family life, the uncertainty of employment and a poisoned environment, is such a religious commitment sufficiently an education to anger? This now venerable institution, and thousands of dedicated teachers who work in it together with the parents who support it, is coming to realise that a bolder imagination is necessary. A 'private school system' without an ethical imagination is being recognised as an anomaly.

On the subject of church schools, Andrew Greeley, in a recent article reflecting on the findings of a recent National Opinion Research Center survey into Catholic schools, underscores their value, precisely when, in recent years, their role had come to be doubted in American society. He writes:

Virtually all the criticisms aimed at the Catholic schools are refuted by these data: They are not rigid, repressive, dull or restrictive. On the contrary they seem to facilitate greater happiness, more support for the equality of women, more confidence in other people, more willingness to see sex as a sacrament, greater generosity to the church, more benign images of God, greater awareness of the complexity of moral decision making, and higher intellectual achievement. Not bad.[28]

He admits both his agreeable surprise at such results, and the likelihood that those opposed to Catholic schools will be not be affected by such data. His conclusion is, predictably challenging:

But, God willing, I shall continue to purchase space for the church school question in the General Social Survey so that the splendid twilight of the Catholic schools can be recorded for posterity. Thus, historians of the future can marvel at how foolish we were to give up because of loss of nerve or loss of faith what might have been our best resource. Catholic schools, after all, were the answer.[29]

To speak more generally, there must be room for something more. If the extent of our moral imagination is exhausted in condemning smoking, in promoting random breath tests and advertising campaigns against AIDS, has morality become mere cost-effectiveness? Beyond what conservative groups call permissiveness and liberal elements call freedoms, is there a moral centre of any kind? If we cannot find a way of talking about the fundamental violence of abortion, of unregulated wealth, of the pornographic exploitation of the young, of indiscriminate media-prying into private lives, how are we imagining the way we belong together? With the hardening of the heart comes a darkening of the mind; and in that hardening and darkness, a decomposition of the social imagination.

Decline has a still deeper level. Not only does it compromise and distort progress. Not only do inattention, obtuseness, un-reasonableness, irresponsibility produce objectively absurd situations. Not only do ideologies corrupt minds. But compromise and distortion discredit progress. Objectively absurd situations do not yield to treatment. Corrupt minds have a flair for picking the mistaken solution and insisting that it alone is intelligent, reasonable, good. Imperceptibly the corruptions spreads from the harsh sphere of material advantage and power to the mass media, the stylish journals, the literary movements, the educational process, the reigning philosophies. A civilisation in decline digs its own grave with relentless consistency. It cannot be argued out of its self-destructive ways, for argument has a theoretical premiss, theoretical premisses are asked to conform to matters of fact, and facts in the situation produced by decline more and more are the absurdities that proceed from inattention, oversight, unreasonableness and irresponsibility.[30]

The basic spiritual irony is that a confession of sin releases the soul's forces for something new. As confrontations on particular issues occasionally convulse public discussion, as an exhausted tolerance takes a further step back from the complexity of the issues, we are feeling the need of a new language of moral imagination which will not be deterred by the inane classifications of being progressive or conservative, Left or Right. For what is at stake is the moral centre and the compassionate heart of our possible commonwealth. After all, morality is fundamentally a way of imagining the common good. It envisages a shared wholeness, a centre, before the inevitable classification begins and our sturdy instincts to social conformism take over. Admittedly the egoist in all of us does not turn into an altruist overnight. Mutually hostile groups do not easily forget past grievances and see beyond their resentment and suspicions. But where is a beginning to be made in a healing of memories and the release of a new imagining?

Having a Heart

Fundamental to the permanent poem within is the presence of feeling, 'having a heart'. Without a feeling for what is genuinely human, values simply do not occur in our consciousness. Soured or resentful feelings, unnamed feelings of despair and victimisation, block the development of a more hopeful, open sense of belonging and partnership. Such statements as 'there is no God in the bush', 'the sun killed religion in Australia', express a reciprocity of influence between the inner and outer landscape of our lives, at least in harsher, more tragic times of Australian development. Marcus Clarke, in his preface to Adam Lindsay Gordon's poems, expressed the sense of despairing impotence suffered by those who explored the 'dead heart' of this continent:

> *Hopeless explorers have named them (the mountains) out of their suffering—Mount Misery, Mount Dreadful, Mount Despair..the soul, placed before the frightful grandeur of those barren hills, drinks in their sentiment of defiant ferocity, and is steeped in bitterness.*[31]

The harshness of the outer landscape has its double in the heart. Some poets have explored the inner landscape and the levels of repressed feeling which block the development of moral imagining.

Jim McAuley's poem, 'Because' laments the lack of warmth on the family scene. Though obviously autobiographical, this poem evokes a good deal that is common to the styles of family interaction in the experience of the majority of Australians from English and Celtic backgrounds. 'We were all closed in the same defeat.' The unexpressive relationship between the parents, and the lack of tenderness and spontaneity of the father, the stylised emotion of the mother sweetly singing sentimental songs, is now seen as 'mainly weakness'. The child too was unable to respond. It took its toll. The poet asks why it should matter to him so much, even though he admits it 'bore more hardly on my mother/ Who had more generous feelings to express'. His father 'damned up his Irish blood/ Against all drinking praying fecklessness/ And stiffened into stone and creaking wood'. When the father refuses to kiss the young boy after an absence, the experience 'cut like a saw'. They were good parents, but somehow communicated a desperate lack of feeling to their children. The poet feels such lack of heart affecting his own life in the memorable lines:

> *Judgment is simply trying to reject*
> *A part of what we are because it hurts.*
> *The living cannot call the dead collect:*
> *they won't accept the charge, and it reverts.*
>
> *It's my own judgment day that I draw near,*
> *descending in the past, without a clue,*
> *down to that central deadness: the despair*
> *older than any hope I ever knew.*[32]

The 'central deadness' is fundamental despair. To what degree is this an inherited Australian problem? Such a 'habit of the heart' blocks the radically generous feeling out of which moral imagination arises. It is surely worth asking whether what is most sardonic and abrasive, most knocking in the Australian style has it origins in the sadness of failed family communication.[33] Whatever the answer to such a question, Mary Gilmore offers a genteel solution which, of course, leaves the problem unresolved:

> *Never admit the pain,*
> *Bury it deep;*
> *Only the weak complain,*
> *Complaint is cheap.*
>
> *Cover the wound, fold down*
> *Its curtained place;*
> *Silence is still a crown,*
> *Courage a grace.*[34]

Again she tells us in 'Nurse No Long Grief':

> *O, could we weep,*
> *And weeping bring relief!*
> *But life asks more than tears*
> *And falling leaf.*
>
> *Nurse no long grief,*
> *lest the heart flower no more;*
> *Grief builds no barns; its plough*
> *Rusts at the door.*[35]

These are noble sentiments, rather classical English, the epitome of the stiff upper lip and the desire 'to get on with it'. That such is a part of the Australian psyche can hardly be doubted. But this inability to feel the true pain of our history is exactly what is catching up with us now. It leaves us deprived of compassionate feeling for the other in the special kinds of anguish that afflict society today. AIDS sufferers, single parents abandoned to poverty, urban Aboriginals, the isolated elderly, the young unemployed—all such tell their own stories about the violent exclusion they feel. Hardness of heart obstructs the benevolent flow of social communication: 'Bow, rock, steel, spring,/ Seamed, grained,strained, threaded inside/ Like agony to save your pride.'[36] The harsh individual 'will to power', uncaring about the values that can be felt only in tenderness and compassion, 'destroys the power to will':

The will to power destroys the power to will.
The weapon made, we cannot help but use it;
it drags us with its own momentum still. [37]

Jill Conway has suggested further evidence of this bleak emotional environment. Though she admits that the history of the affective life of Australians is still to be written, such poetic testimony suggests a starting point. A lot of change has taken place, but:

> To the occasional visitor, the continuities seem more profoundly striking. Thus, it seems no accident Australia's recent great out-pouring of achievement in film has reworked the theme of the isolated male hero, and the woman who must reject her sexuality for achievement. They seem larger-than-life figures whether in Technicolor or in the pages of The Bulletin where they first appeared. [38]

Les Murray, in his 'An Absolutely Ordinary Rainbow', [39] offers his criticism of our inability to feel, and suggests the redemptive release that is possible. 'There's a fellow crying in Martin Place. They can't stop him.' The crowd gathers to find this strange event a kind of sacred space, 'the dignity of his weeping holds us back from his space', 'a halo/ or force stood around him'. The tough slick crowd trembles in the silence and 'with unexpected judgments of peace'. They too feel, to their amazement, a 'longing for tears like a child for a rainbow'. Those most at home with this unnerving phenomenon are typically the most defenceless, the most innocent and close to nature, and the feminine:

> ...Only the smallest children
> and such as look out of Paradise come near him
> and sit at his feet, with dogs and dusty pigeons.
>
> and I see a woman, shining, stretch her hand
> and shake as she receives the gift of weeping,
> as many as follow her receive the gift receive it.

The man, to the poet, is evidently a 'Christ figure' offering a special kind of Australian redemption in the heart of Sydney. 'But the weeping man, like the earth, requires nothing', as he cries out:

not words, but grief, not messages, but sorrow
hard as the earth, sheer, present as the sea—
and when he stops, he simply walks between us
mopping his face with the dignity of one
man who has wept, and now has finished weeping.

Subtle allusions to the gospel at once invite Christian con-science to find a redemptive meaning here, but also pass a pithy judgment on our unfeeling religion. 'Evading believers, he hurries off down Pitt Street.'

The ethical imagination begins with 'having a heart'. It expands when the power to feel, lost in the anonymous urban technopolis which has become the immediate environment of most of our lives, is recovered. A heart capable of being healed of such diseased and fragmented individualism is presumed in any social morality. For the reality of solidarity is founded on a kind of compassionate intersubjectivity. The 'common good' is not primarily a computerised generalisation. It is first of all a common feeling. The transcendent focus of faith places such solidarity, and such common feeling, in an ultimately personal and benevolent universe. No doubt there are religious resour-ces that remain to be tapped. For the Christian notion of God implies, at its deepest, the mystery of corporate mutual belong-ing:

No man has ever seen God; if we love one another, God abides in
us and his love is perfected is us... he who does not love his brother
whom he has seen, cannot love God whom he has not seen. (I Jn
4:12,20)

The Prayer of Compassion

Bruce Dawe expresses how prayer expands into touching com-passion and solidarity with the suffering. In his 'Prayer for those in Coma',[40] he skilfully exploits the image of survivors from a torpedoed ship to express a spiritual belonging to those who are most helpless. They embody our common human plight. He prays to the God who alone can help the totally helpless:

Lord, for those mariners adrift
on pain's equivocal ocean,
be the buoy bobbing on the water's waste,
the hope of landfall as they listless lie

> *in the body's open boat, feverishly chewing*
> *the salt-soaked leather of words for sustenance.*

His prayer makes him ask the restoration of such sufferers to the human world to which they maintain only the most tenuous bonds:

> *Restore to them*
> *the world that foundered when the blind*
> *torpedo took them below the waterline, that world*
> *whose ghostly aftermath is these*
> *white laundered shapes that creak like gulls,*
> *like gulls in search of communicability's scraps*
> *among the floating debris and the oil slick...*

The poem turns from the consideration of the pitiable condition of the helpless to our ambiguous and uneven solidarity in the human condition—all sinners, *nobis quoque peccatoribus*, all sailors, be it under a neutral flag or in true commitment to our neighbour. The same tragic possibilities are common to all. They are brought to mind in the contemplation of the actual tragedy of the sufferers, who, though locatable within our world of experience, are eerily removed and apart from it: 'the same submarine wolf-pack closes in':

> *Nobis quoque peccatoribus—*
> *We are all sailors if it comes to that,*
> *whether its under a neutral flag, or flying*
> *the aggressive ensign of life-long commitment*
> *—still the same submarine wolfpack closes in,*
> *and tin fish carve a white path through the waves.*

The prayer of compassion becomes precise. The ultimate mystery in which we belong is invoked, even if our own individual small worlds of isolated pain prevent its identification:

> *Lord, whom our coma helps us not to see,*
> *these men are tired and weary of the sea.*

Prayer in Action

If Dawe's poem is a prayer expressing and asking for a deeper compassion, Lesbia Harford's 'Poem LXXIV'[41] expresses an active compassion opening out to prayer. The 'aggressive ensign of life-long commitment' is presumed. What is at stake is the transcendent significance of this commitment to the human. The poem is written from an agnostic stance, a somewhat typical position in the public life of Australia. While acknowledging a Christian inheritance, the poet feels incapable of articulating it with any conviction:

> *I am no mystic. All the ways of God*
> *Are dark to me;*
> *I know not if he lived or if he died*
> *In agony.*

Here the religious tone is fundamentally humanist. Authentic life is the business of meeting human needs. That is the obvious reality, and the human response to it the most evident of spiritual obligations:

> *My every act has reference to man;*
> *Some human need*
> *Of this one, or of that, of myself*
> *Inspires the deed.*

Yet the poet is aware of the presence of a religious tradition. It appears in the exotic form of 'the dim, incanted words' of 'a Latin prayer'. She hopes that they might express a larger meaning, the dim words shining into larger dimensions, a larger space of life.

> *But when I hear the Angelus, I say*
> *A Latin prayer,*
> *Hoping the dim, incanted words may shine*
> *Some way, somewhere.*

The possibility is that this larger meaning of the universe will be disclosed, and, in her case, repossessed. The pragmatic 'ethics' of meeting human needs leads to a hope of participating in a moral universe. Humanism looks to an ultimate and universal Love:

> *Words and a will may work upon my mind*
> *Till ethics turn*
> *To that transcendent love with which*
> *The seraphim burn.*

The poet leaves us there. Our decent, human commitments pose the question of their ultimate foundation.

Vulnerable Values

Bicentenary Australia finds us examining our conscience as a nation. We are aware of a loss of innocence in our moral history. This is occurring at a time when the enormous moral challenges confronting society tend to make for a sad inventory of our moral resources. For a politician to break out of the usual rhetoric of economic management or adversarial warfare into something approaching moral persuasion, is a risk. There are no votes in a larger view. For such a vision, of its nature tends often to be centrist, inviting to reconciliation, rather than appealing to the partisan. Further, the Australian conscience, our 'permanent poem' is not that of an innocent self in an angelic world, but that of a national identity unfolding in a history ridden with conflicts and ambiguities. Disillusionment, let down, all the irresolvable collisions of world views we now clinically term 'pluralism', affect national awareness with apprehension about 'the way things are going'. The truly valuable is always vulnerable; and the higher the values the more vulnerable they are to cynical dismissal. The 'real world' is more easily manipulable, it would seem, by the shapers of *Realpolitik* than by the peacemakers. It is more hospitable to the exploiters of the human—those who peddle drugs or pornography or fiddle with our national resources, than to the promoters of the human, in education, art or religion. It is more susceptible to sleazy compromises in the high places of government, the judiciary, law enforcement, unions and the professions, than to desirable reforms in any of these areas. It is more apt to express a sudden and rigid legalism in dealings with Aboriginal rights, rather than risk anything resembling national reconciliation with these original inhabitants of the land by resolutely diagnosing the crimes of the past and the present.

A Costigan or Fitzgerald Royal Commission have fed the public mind with a steady diet of instances of moral failure. To name the crimes that have been committed, to identify and immobilise the true offenders, to prescribe and implement reforms will demand an excess of dedication and energy. To envision a commonwealth where such perversion of justice is not the order of the day seems to defy the imagination. The troubling question is how to turn the rout into a rally. Evan Jones' poem[42] is oddly prescient as he deals with 'The Point':

The point, I imagine, is
not to learn to expect
betrayal, self-deceit, lies
however thick they collect
in the cul-de-sac of one's days,
half-noticed, half-numbered, half-checked:
but rather to learn to praise
fidelity, trust and love
which in their modest ways
continue to be and move
(however mocked, however derided,
however difficult, indeed, to prove)
utterly undivided—
if inarticulate or mute,
still mortally decided.

'The Point' can, in a typically Australian manner, be 'inarticulate', 'mute'. It is a matter of not being overwhelmed by the individual or social problem of evil 'betrayal, self-deceit, lies' collecting in the dead ends of our national history. The point, rather, resides in a liberated openness to the world of values which are the momentum and direction of authentic human life, no matter how 'unreal' they appear to be in the 'real world' of the cynic, the power hungry, the exploiter and the criminal. Such a horizon of self-transcending commitment does not put one in a world of genteel respectability or social acceptance. It is a horizon, at one boundary occupied by the prophet, the martyr; at the other, by millions of unnamed human beings whose unrecognised goodness holds the world together in a life-giving conspiracy. Without such daily self-transcendence for the sake of what is genuinely worthwhile, any society drifts into harshness and triviality:

Neither fashionable nor astute,
this point to take to heart:
merely final and absolute:
without it, no people, no life, no art.

Again, we touch on a fundamental question for the church: how does it locate itself in Australian culture and society? As Lonergan notes, 'a religion that promotes self-transcendence to the point not merely of justice, but of self-sacrificing love, will have a redemptive role in human society inasmuch as such love can undo the mischief of decline and restore the cumulative process of progress'.[43] In other words, faith is always the promise of a new beginning: in place of the experience of the world as absurd, it cultivates a gracious vision of ultimate love and providence. The hope that it inspires is not defeated by despair over failure, past or present. The charity it inspires demands forgiveness of past wrongs and self-forgetfulness in moving forward into a future from which no one may be excluded.[44]

Imagining the Other

James McAuley, in his 'One Thing at Least'[45] focuses on the summit of such moral commitment in the instance of loving another. Any spirituality manifests its genuineness in such practical loving. At root, it has to mean a continuing education of 'the heart', the classic Western symbol of the depth of one's feeling, the individuality of one's freedom, the definiteness of one's commitments.

> One thing at least I understood
> Practically from the start,
> that loving must be learned by heart
> If its to be any good.

The turn in the church's consciousness toward the poor and the underprivileged, the nation's new awareness of injustices inflicted on Aboriginals, any new social disposition to welcome refugees, the beginnings of good feelings about the possibility of another kind of Australia on a more humanly comprehensive scale, all end in the need to deepen perceptions, to educate ourselves to a new vision and to implement our commitments 'if its to be any good'. McAuley goes on to reflect:

> It isn't in the flash of thunder,
> But in the silent power to give—
> A habit into which we live
> Ourselves and grow to be a wonder.

The great Australian 'silence' has to become, in this sense, 'the silent power to give', a new consciousness of being for the other. It might be expected that this radical dispossession will be in terms of a newsworthy 'flash of thunder', a media event of unprecedented scale starring all the *dramatis personae* at home in such happenings. Rather, what is at stake is how we begin to possess ourselves and educate our feeling and freedom in the deepest disposition of our lives ('a habit'). It is something that cannot be done for us. It comes about, as it were, 'from the inside out'. It is a new awareness of radical creativity, that of self-giving: in biblical terms, the heart of stone becomes the heart of flesh.

The habit expressing itself in 'the silent power to give' with all its intimations of personal transformation ('grow to be a wonder') has still to be reconciled to human reality. It is a slow process of learning and education. Egoists do not become altruists overnight. The world of values, though stubbornly persistent, remains oddly elusive in the hurried pragmatism of life. The poet speaks for us all:

> *Some like me are slow to learn:*
> *What's plain can be mysterious still.*

Conflicts sour good feelings and easy enthusiasms. Old prejudices, be they national, cultural, racial or religious in origin, return. Historical resentments deeply mark any character, individual or national. The constant point is the ever-new decision to be for the other(s). True value, not self-gratification, sustains such a conversion. This transcends the ebb and flow of feeling. Or, better, it invites the deepest level of feeling to emerge as a kind of radical passion. In it one decides what is worth living for, and how one should relate to the other, and to society itself:

> *Feelings alter, fade, return*
> *But love stands constant in the will:*
> *It's not alone the touching, seeing,*
> *It's how to mean the other's being.*

The challenge confronting us at this point of our history is how to occupy the heart of Australia.[46] It is there that the quality of life is being formed. It is in the heart, new-found or new- possessed, that Australia becomes not just a natural habitat but a human place. We are not without our prophets pointing to this kind of exploration. The Catholic bishops have initiated their wealth enquiry. Dozens of communities, new and old, without too many words and no public recognition, are struggling to begin something different. The witness of Aboriginal Australians to another way of being here continues.

Manning Clark has initiated an inspired re-telling of the Australian story, as have our artists, our poets. The words of one of the seminal thinkers of our age, Bernard Lonergan, point to the continual 'happening' of the new, inviting all to join in a more hopeful national experiment:

> *It is as though a room was filled with music though one can have no sure knowledge of its source. There is in the world, as it were, a charged field of love and meaning; here and there it reaches a notable intensity: but it is ever unobtrusive, hidden, inviting us to join. And join we must if we are to perceive it, for our perceiving is through our loving.* [47]

---

1. John Bryson in 'Does Australia have a soul?', *Bulletin*, March 28, 1989, p. 95.

2. Richard Kearney, *The Wake of the Imagination*, p. 365.

3. Les Murray, *Embodiment...*, pp. 22–23.

4. Robert Bellah, *The Broken Covenant*, Seabury, New York, 1976, p. 162.

5. C. M. H. Clark, *A History of Australia*, Volumes I–VI, Melbourne University Press, 1962–1987.

6. See Hugh Collins, 'Political Ideology in Australia', *Australia...*, p. 159. For a critical comment on Manning Clark's project, Bruce N. Kaye, 'Manning Clark's Interpretation of Religion in Australia', *ANZ...Religious History*, pp. 93–112. This strikes me as both fair and positive.

7. See Moira Eastman's *Family. The Vital Factor. The Key to Society's Survival*, Collins Dove, Melbourne, 1989. This book is an outstanding resource in discussing the meaning and the role of the family, especially since it is not marked by any reactionary bias. For statistics on government expenditure, see pp. 102–106.

8. For statistics and further comment see *Australia Unveiled. The Changing Face of a Nation*, Peter Smark and Judith Whelan (eds.) *Age* Publications, Melbourne, 1989, pp. 2–3.

9. Distinguished Australian scientist, Charles Birch, 'Embracing the Future', in Andrew Dutney (ed.), *From Here to Where?*, Uniting Church Press, Melbourne, 1988, pp. 110–111, expresses the larger problem:

> *In our present frame of mind, we measure the health of our nation by the rate of its economic growth in material goods. The idea is that an increase in the material standard of living is good and that it is to be achieved primarily by increasing the goods that people consume. But the 'growth equals welfare' equation no longer holds. It begs the question of what sort of goods are really needed, and who needs them most. And we leave to the last to question the effect of our economic activities on the environment that sustains the economy. Somehow we have to disengage ourselves from that stranglehold.*

10.   John Carroll, 'Mateship and Egalitarianism: The Failure of Upper Middle Class Nerve', in John Carroll (ed.), *Intruders in the Bush. The Australian Quest for Identity*, Oxford University Press, Melbourne, 1982, pp. 143–156.

11.   Hugh Stretton, 'The Quality of Leading Australians', in *Australia...*, p. 220.

12.   Hugh Stretton, 'The Quality...', p. 224.

13.   That the present government should share the same concerns as the Catholic bishops is well indicated in David O'Reilly's, 'Retreat Australia Fair', *The Bulletin*, April 25, 1989, pp. 52–60.

14.   Nicholas Jose, *Australia...*, p. 314.

15.   S. R. Graubard, *Australia...*, pp. viii–ix.

16.   Hugh Collins, 'Political ideology in Australia', *Australia...*, p. 157.

17.   Collins, 1985, p. 163.

18.   On this point, see the work of an Australian moral philosopher, Norman Ford, *When did I begin? Conception of the Human Individual in History, Philosophy and Science*, Cambridge University Press, 1988.

19.   Donald Horne, 'Who rules Australia?', *Australia...*, p. 182.

20.   How the church can re-imagine itself in Australian society is provocatively suggested in Denis Edward's valuable little book, *Called to be Church in Australia*, St Paul Publications, Homebush, 1987.

21.   Richard J. Neuhaus, *The Catholic Moment. The Paradox of the Church in the Postmodern World*, Harper and Row, San Francisco, 1987.

22.   Neuhaus, 1987, p. 282.

23.   Taken from *Method in Theology* by Bernard Lonergan, published and copyright 1972 by Darton, Longman and Todd Ltd. and used by permission of the publishers.

24.   See Michael Mason, 'Yesterday's Failure of Nerve and Today's Fear of Flying', *Compass Theology Review* 23, Summer, 1988, pp. 15–21.

25.   *Method...*, p. 54.

26.   A MacIntyre, *After Virtue*, University of Notre Dame Press, 1981.

27.   Harper and Row, New York, 1986.

28.   Andrew Greeley, 'Catholic Schools: A Golden Twilight?', *America*, 11 February, 1989, p. 116.

29.   Greeley, p. 118.

30.   Lonergan, *Method...*, p. 55.

31.   Quoted by Judith Wright, 'Landscape and Dreaming', *Australia...*, p. 52.

32.   James McAuley, *A Map of Australian Verse*, Oxford University Press, Melbourne, 1975, pp. 214–215.

33.   See Ronald Conway, *The End of Stupor*, Sun Books, Melbourne, 1984, especially 'The Unquiet Cradle', pp. 18–46.

34.   *Anthology...*, p. 100. Reprinted from *Selected Verse,* © *The Estate of Dame Mary Gilmore, 1948, by permission of Angus & Robertson Publishers/Collins.*

35.   James McAuley (ed.), *A Map of Australian Verse*, Oxford University Press, Melbourne, 1975, p. 91.

36.   David Rowbotham, 'Stoic', *Anthology...*, p. 99.

37.   Judith Wright, 'Weapon', *Anthology...*, p. 99. Reprinted from *Collected Poems 1942–70,* © Judith Wright, 1971, by permission of Angus & Robertson Publishers/Collins.

38.   Jill Conway, 'Gender in Australia', *Australia...*, p. 366. A valuable resource for such a history of affectivity is Ron Conway's *The End of Stupor*, together with his other writings.

39.   *Anthology...*, p. 100. Reprinted from *The Vernacular Republic Poems 1961–81,* © Les A. Murray, 1982, by permission of Angus & Robertson Publishers/Collins.

40.   *Anthology...*, p. 272. Reprinted from *Condolences of the Season*, Longman Cheshire, 1971, by permission of the publisher.

41.   *Anthology...*, p. 280.

42.   *Anthology...*, p. 263. Reprinted from *Recognitions*, ANU Press, 1978, by permission of the publisher.

43.   *Method...*, p. 55.

44.   There must be some way to overcome what David O'Reilly, *Intelligencer*, May, 1989, p. 5, has called 'The Hatred Factor'. Recent events in the Liberal Party occasioned his reflections, though he sees this demoralising feature in all aspects of politics. He concludes,

> *But let's not kid around. Blind hatred is often the engine of politics... Hatred is driving the combatants in all this. The danger is that they hate so hard and wait so long to settle old scores that they become caricatures of hate. Politics is demeaned, because people are not fools.*

One of the most intriguing and unexplored aspects of modern history is 'the forgiveness factor': this is always the pre-condition for any radically new imagining—the European Common Market is an instructive example.

45.   *Anthology...*, p. 262. Reprinted from *Collected Poems 1936–70,* © *Norma McAuley, 1971, by permission of Angus & Robertson Publishers/Collins.*

46.   See *A New Heart for a New World*, St Paul Publications, 1986.

47.   *Method...*, p. 290.

Chapter 4: The Australian Conversation: Do our Minds ever Meet?

'...the approaching tide of technological revolution in the atomic age could so captivate, bewitch, dazzle and beguile man that calculative thinking may someday come to be accepted and practiced as the only way of thinking.

What great danger then might move upon us? Then there might go hand in hand with the greatest ingenuity in calculative planning and inventing an indifference toward meditative thinking, total thoughtlessness. And then? Then man would have denied and thrown away his own special nature—that he is a meditative being. Therefore the issue is saving man's essential nature. Therefore, the issue is keeping meditative thinking alive.' (Martin Heidegger)[1]

Here I am relating spirituality to having a mind capable of 'wholespeak' conversation. It would mean a mind free to imagine the scope of the possible, by not foreclosing on the transcendent possibilities of faith in whatever form it occurs. It must also mean a mind capable of hitting on strategies of resistance to what threatens or stunts such human possibilities. It has to mean a readiness to search beyond the economy into the whole ecology of life, beyond mere quantity to the quality of our lives, to press beyond the image to the real, beyond the mask to the human face, to break out of an alienated individualism into the horizon of cosmic and social belonging. Most of all, it is to cultivate a spirit that loses neither its humour nor its capacity to wonder, despite the cataract of problems that inundate human awareness today.

Unfortunately, 'spirituality' often connotes a rather soft-headed approach to the real—delicate feelings, devout affections, a disengagement of intellect, being busy with another world. Yet the contention of this chapter is that true spirituality fosters a genuine intellectual quest. Conversion to the ultimate dimension not only gives a basis for a more hopeful, inclusive social morality; it also stimulates a more playful conversation about what is most meaningful in our lives together. It sets free the imagination to be at once ethical and poetic. If theology, to refer to a venerable axiom, is 'faith seeking understanding', spirituality is the intimations of such faith looking for its 'wholespeak' in ways that nourish both the ethical and the poetic imagination.

The Closing of the Australian Mind?

The earliest philosophical and theological thinkers were familiar with the plight of the soul that rejects its aspirations to the transcendent and the whole. Such a flight from reality resulted in both a hardening of the heart and a darkening of the mind. If the previous chapter explored some of the problems of the Australian 'heart', this one looks to the problems of intelligence Down Under, or, more generally, to the intellectual problems of the Australian imagination.

Sir Karl Popper once raised the question of whether our world was in such a mess because human beings were very wicked or very stupid. He was inclined to think that the latter was the case. For the modern world has abounded in intense moralities of one kind or another. When these are divorced from the imaginative and critical mind, things go wrong. The original social morality of Marxism ended in the Gulag. Liberalism with all its high aspirations to personal freedom and revolutionary energy led to a capitalist monopoly of the world's resources, and their subsequent exhaustion. Powerful trade unions bonded in a solidarity originating in the British class warfare of the last century, have reached a point at which they are notably insensitive to the crises of unemployment affecting our society generally and to the fragility of the international networks of our economy. Any morality, however liberating in intention, without an intellectual sense of proportion, once it has lost its imagination, becomes repressive—at least in its inability to imagine reality beyond the confines of individual or group interest.

It is this kind of problem that should give us pause. Patrick White remarks on our lack of ironic intelligence in reference to recent national celebrations: '…a large proportion of grown Australians remain children at heart—I see them as kidults. That's why they're so easily deceived by politicians, developers, organisers of festivals, and that is why they fail to dig the real purpose of a giant circus like the Bi.'[2] It makes you suspect that our primary problem is the lack of a philosophy. For where do we find in our culture the 'love for wisdom' once so prized as the goal of the searching soul? The disenchanted technological world of our pragmatism is now a plastic-wrapped inability to feel for what is really going on. The face of the suffering other is reduced to a negative indicator in a computer printout. Our spiritual disharmony is starkly symbolised in the destruction of so much of our environment. Do we really know what to do with the inspired voices among us? How does our truth include the astringent vision of a Patrick White, the deep human sensibilities of a Manning Clark, the deeper intuitions of the feminist turn in our culture, our newly found ecological awareness, the cultural criticism of newly articulate Aboriginal voices, the multicultural diversity with us now, the fundamental witness of great religious traditions among us?

Heirs of a flatly secular culture, now largely bankrupt, our public language is stunted to the point of being grotesque. What larger imagination remains when the only solution to the drug problem appears to many to be legalisation, when the main strategy against the AIDS epidemic is more available condoms, when the only answer to the crises of education is more government-imposed uniformity, and when the main solution to the plight of the growing number of the poor and homeless in our country is to deregulate the activities of the very rich?

If Patrick White refers so scathingly to our 'kidult' propensities, most commentators at least recognise as evident a special kind of anti-intellectualism in our culture. The lament is familiar: 'Over there' is where intelligence really happens; Australia is the experimental station for discarded theories; the ten-year gap between the acceptance of ideas abroad and their arrival in Australia. Such laments express, at least, implicitly, our failure to imagine our own situation in all its possibilities and predicaments.[3] Even in regard to the European and North American theologies of recent decades proclaiming such new directions as the cultural 'Death of God', the triumph of the secular, 'the Theology of Hope', or, more recently, 'liberation theology', we have taken a lot of time to realise that Australians have experienced the cultural absence of God, the presence of a massively established secularism, the oppression of isolation and despair, long before such matters were discovered 'over there'! Even the noble attempts of South American theologians of Liberation can be uncritically imported without an accompanying realisation that our basic problem is one of oppression of spirit. The most urgent liberation we need is that of mind. When our intellectual authorities reside elsewhere, our local suspicion of elites (except in sport) does not favour independent questioning. Sustained critical reflection is not listed among our national pastimes! The judgment on such a mentality is best encapsulated in the Russian proverb, 'a fish rots first in the head'.

While there is at present a remarkable interest in what is distinctively Australian (excessive in the judgment of some), intelligence so often tends to be an imported reality. Summing up this tradition of imported intelligence, Dame Leonie Kramer writes:

> ...there is little understanding of whether or how they [such ideas] will be adapted to Australian conditions. The reason is that Australia still lacks a rigorous, constructive critical tradition. It is no accident that the word 'knocking' has come to be recognised as an accurate term for a negative Australian habit of derogatory dismissal of an idea or an achievement. There is a tendency to argue from extreme positions and to question the status of objectivity...The general weakness in the practice of criticism is evidenced both in the ready acceptance of the latest doctrine, and in the tendency for criticism to be taken personally...in spite of efforts to correct the so called 'cultural cringe', there is still an inclination to deal with local writers tenderly; and for some of them to respond to criticism with indignation or peevishness.[4]

The reasons for this persistent lack of intellectual self-confidence in Australian life are still elusive. Educational opportunity has expanded greatly in the last forty years. Perhaps we failed to notice sufficiently that, being natively pragmatic and utilitarian, certain styles of 'progressive education' feed our lack of intellectual concern and 'soften the rigour of learning'.[5]

The question that aches beneath Australian culture concerns the very meaning of education: education to what? One suspects that discussion of our philosophy of education, or lack of it, is most likely to throw light on our cultural state of mind. Today, this is especially the case. The strong government push to make education, above all tertiary education, an instrument of economic recovery is having a predictable result. The 'softer subjects' are made to move over to make room for the hard sciences of quantifiable value in the future economy. Education is not seen as promoting the unfolding of a consciousness exploring its place in the universe, nor the ability to enter imaginatively into the largest possible social and political conversation, but the skill to slot into the big factory of Australia Inc.

If some have thought that Australia suffers from the fear of the open spaces of the mind, such a judgment must be placed in a larger, comparative context. For example, there is the American case. To give one example, Alan Bloom's *The Closing of the American Mind: How higher education has failed democracy and impoverished the souls of today's students*[6] laments a state that we never even reached! The general thesis of the book is indicated well enough in its title. It is 'a meditation on the state of our souls...' from the standpoint of a distinguished American teacher and scholar. It is a piercingly critical book as it laments the decline of the structures of liberal education in the USA: the great human concerns encapsulated in the Socratic 'know thyself' have been replaced by a fragmented and superficial specialisation. Indeed, if Bloom is correct in his critique, education has become a distraction from the great human questions rather than an introduction to them. The general malaise can best be described as fragmentation. It has become a matter of offering more and more about less and less.[7]

Of course, Bloom has in mind the enormous institution of US college education. It is a critique of an institution that does not exist, or does not yet exist, here. On the other hand, Australian tertiary education is arguably even more specialised than the North American version. One can only hope that some kind of similar Australian critique of the closing of the Australian mind will be forthcoming. In the meantime we have to live with the possibility that the Australian mind was never 'opened' by a critical liberal tradition before it was closed. That, naturally, is a longer story. What can concern us, however, is the quality of conversation about things of the spirit: on this level do our minds ever meet? Is the larger imagination of life being dropped from our national conversation—even organised out of it? Has there been a foreclosure on the scope of human imagining? The times tend to run into a kind of inverted millenarianism. Not an imminent utopia but an impending doom is the sense of the future. Is education cutting the coming generations off from their most hopeful resources?[8] If 'imagination is the irrepressible revolutionist' (Wallace Stevens), have we been busy repressing it? If 'the slow fuse of the possible is lit by the imagination' (Emily Dickinson), are we set, not for the explosion of new hope, but for quietly fizzling desperation?

Qualities of Mind

I would suggest that there are three obvious qualities of mind in Australian culture. The first is the most positive: space; the second is the most ambiguous: a wilderness of images; the third is the most noticeable: intellectual apartheid. A word on each of these.

Space

Australia *does* enjoy some intellectual advantage, even if, compared with overseas intellectual styles, our style of learning is cooler. We can be detached from the intense, often dramatic, dialectics of European thinking. We are spared the novelties of quick-shifting North American fashions of thought. This need not mean cultural isolation. It may even mean a more healthy receptivity. For here a variety of ideas have a chance to swirl around out of their pressurised containers and come back to earth under their own weight. Wave after wave of intellectual excitement from Europe and the USA, the exotic 'in thing', the 'radical critique', the 'new wave', break on the shore of this continent often in more sober forms. What was inherently worthwhile in the original impetus survives to find a place in a more spacious and less excited intellectual climate. It might be, if we realised it, that by not being locked into overseas intellectual movements we have the opportunity to cultivate a more spacious imagination. A larger vision is being offered us, perhaps even a wisdom, something distinctive to ourselves. Here the extreme, mutually exclusive positions of other climes have a chance of meeting in a larger centre. The Left and Right wings of so much contemporary debate have a chance of being joined in a body. Overseas 'black and white' debates can resolve in a larger play of colours.

I have often been impressed with how, at least in the disciplines with which I am familiar and with regard to the countries I know, Australians are far more likely to be open to British, German, French, North American ideas in a way that is not remarkable in their places of origin. There, intellectual opinion is far more the victim of national language and culture than it is here. You might say that this is because our national culture is not as dramatically engaging as the more complex cultures of Europe and the USA. We are less anchored, more free to pick and choose and to range wider. What we lack in intensity we gain in extent. Conversation on the larger human realities can have its unique flavour precisely because of our cultural non-alignment. Our continent, and the culture it nourishes, provide an openness that promises its own value. Distance is not always a tyranny, especially given today's opportunities for travel and information exchange. The question is, of course, whether we will be prepared to profit from our situation.[9]

A Wilderness of Images

Here the situation is marked with special ambiguity. Though the eminent French philosopher, Paul Ricoeur, has stressed the importance of the image in human knowledge in his oft-quoted axiom, 'the symbol gives rise to thought',[10] our problem seems to be otherwise. For an exuberant symbolism pervades the Australian mind, especially when it comes to issues of national identity. The danger is that such symbols have been too naively assimilated. By not being sufficiently critical about them, our thinking has been blocked in its development to a more broad and inclusive scope. The history of our literature recognises so many such symbols, myths and images as Tom Inglis Moore has documented.[11] They tend, however, to congeal into a slogan, or fixate in an image of a repressive or noble past without allowing for the full range of our experience. Have we, one wonders, been sufficiently iconoclastic about ourselves?

It is significant that we have been highly productive of images about ourselves precisely at a time when the culture of the mass-produced image is dominant. Instead of being the play of imagination to suggest new ways of feeling about and for our society, such images are formed into a collage of skilfully packaged and highly commercialised versions of what Australians are supposed to be. What we *are* is anyone's guess! What we might become, at a new time in our history, is removed to the domain of hope.

In the modern world of late capitalism, the image has become a consumer item. As such, it does not suggest any new creativity. It functions within an ideology of empty and un-thinking imitation. Not only does the image sell; it has become what we want to buy. It is the way we choose to appear. More and more, the image is the reality. In the larger human scope, such images conceal rather than reveal what we are. In the inflation of image which modern communication promotes, social conscience is distorted: human contact becomes public relations; values happen to be what is most advertised; the worth of the person is his or her ability to buy an image, the right car, the right house, the right suburb, perhaps increasing-ly, the right country. We are not all 'Crocodile Dundees', not all 'Men from Snowy River', not all 'good mates', a 'weird mob', 'Ockers'—nor Dame Ednas, nor Con the Fruiterer, for that matter.[12]

Les A. Murray makes a similar point in a recent essay.[13] You can compile an endless list of images about Australia itself: the Australian Emptiness, the Lucky Country, the Land of the Long Weekend, the Great Australian Stupor, the End of Dreamtime, the Tyranny of Distance, White Australia, the Workingman's Paradise, the Empty Continent, the Sunburnt Soul, the Dead Heart, Gallipoli, Eureka, the Last Frontier... In our apprecia-tion of the image, we tend to forget it is a symbol of a larger reality, the reality of an often suffering 'other' in our midst. The result is that we are tending to buy myths about ourselves which, if they are illuminating at all, need to be critically re-appropriated in a new way. Intelligent irony, intent on a larger imagination, is the only way out of all this. To refuse such a larger critical space is to end in taking ourselves too seriously. Our irony must reach into everything, including ourselves!

You could object that it is the function of art to keep our basic symbols and images alive and healthy. Of course this is correct. On the other hand, it has to contend with the enormous commercialisation of art. The point is well made by Australian art critic, Robert Hughes even though he does not have our own situation precisely in mind. He writes: 'Works of art, once meant to stand apart from the realm of bourgeois luxury and to display their flinty resistance to Capitalist values are now the most eagerly sought and highly paid for'.[14] Because the art is owned by the very rich, it does not follow that the artist is owned—no more than writers with government literature grants are expected to tout the ideology of the current government. Yet the possibility of 'flinty resistance' does become a small but nagging question. Where is it really coming from? Is it projected onto our greater painters and then somehow domesticated in our economy? Or do we have to go deeper: is art more an activity than an object, something resident potentially in the imagination of all human beings in their aspirations for a more spiritual existence? In this series of reflections I have tended to give poetry the privileged place. I have done this precisely because it is of the highest quality, yet, since it has such a humble role in Australian culture, it is the least owned by anyone, and so more apt to confront everyone.

Intellectual apartheid

Less dramatically described than in the above heading, our national conversation lacks the 'meeting of minds'. This is where the space referred to above runs out. We tend to regard someone of different views the way a customs officer might view a traveller suspected of contraband, or an immigration official look at a dubious passport. We are short on open spaces here. We see the mask but not the face. Almost without exception our media interviewers set up any public conversation along adversarial lines, or adopt such a posture themselves.[15] How much room is there for any of us to learn, to change our minds, to come to a more inclusive point of view? Surely human wholeness eludes any one of us or any group of us. The hint of something larger is the outcome of the play of good conversation. It is the occasion of the best kind of humour. But it seems to be that here, for all our abilities to mock or knock or create wonderful irony, we tend to lack a certain kind of intellectual play.

The result, naturally, is that our public discourse becomes increasingly intent on opposition and the problems of disagreement. In an all but absolute manner, it is tyrannised by the metaphor of 'left wing/right wing'. What may have been a natural designation of the seating arrangements in France's First National Assembly two hundred years ago, has become fossilised in the complexities of present-day discourse. We need to imagine the human conversation in a more inclusive manner.[16]

Such rigid polarisation defers a comprehension of the issues. Thus it often increases the problems it seeks to address. A kind of responsibility overload, with associated feelings of pervasive guilt, is the result. We become increasingly problem-ridden people in an exponentially problematic world. And the more the energies of a censorious single-issue mentality convulse social communication, without a sense of the whole, without a centre from which to begin and to which to return, the more we become a society of problem people: problem children of problem parents in a problematic society. When the problematic character of the world is dominant, any genuine collaboration becomes impossible. Not having the instant solution looks like admitting technical incompetence. For we define ourselves only in our terms of our social roles and competences without the saving irony of being something more. Collaboration is at best adversarial warfare. Any deep critique of our culture, with its implied criticism of all our social assumptions, becomes impossible. Laughter, instead of being an earthy admission of our common humanity, becomes simply derision. On the other hand, to the degree that a more spiritual imagination evokes images of radical responsibility in society, it also enables us to laugh together. For it is the wholesome recognition that no one of us is the centre of the universe: 'it needs to be able to laugh with the other as well as to suffer'.[17]

There are signs of a growing disgust with the harshness of partisan projection on the political level marked. Here, as Donald Horne remarks, we experience 'adversarial warfare of the crassest kind'.[18] The partisan mentality of black and white seems to have forgotten the other colours of the spectrum where the possible human resides. Indeed, Don Aitkin regretfully concludes that, for Australians, party alignment is a function of 'habit' rather than of 'understanding'. It has become an excuse not to imagine alternatives. The Westminster system has here fallen on rocky ground. Instead of being the play of politics organised to get the best out of the political conversation, the two-party system has become a fundamentalism of blind political faiths. Partisanship, as Hugh Collins observes, so often congeals into a habit:

> ...*because there is so little to understand: the competitors are offering only slightly different brews of the same ideological ingredients. Because the basic values are similar, the party competition characteristically focuses on tactics and motives rather than on strategies and goals. Since in practical operation the parties are so alike, the rhetoric used by each side typically strains to present the rival in the image of the most extreme and impotent faction.*[19]

This is equivalent to saying that our political life is suffering from a 'narrowspeak' of a most extreme kind. It is a symptom of diseased imagination. A neurotic 'reaction syndrome' blocks fresh understanding or a more comprehensive vision of the whole. Irony fails. If the censorious puritanism of the wowser or the nostalgic lamentations of the social critic lack the spaciousness of something more, so too does our political discourse. One cannot but suspect that it is high time for a politics of humour.

The range of 'wholespeak' of our great national poem, the language of this 'something more', is, I have been contending, the outcome of an intelligence intent on wisdom and the soul's imagination. It is not unlike the language of the dream. There, the ordinary barriers and divisions which structure routine life no longer operate. It works in the psychological context of a wholeness struggling for expression, struggling often against disowned or repressed parts of the persona. It is characterised by the elusive inclusiveness of both/and rather than by polarisations of either/or. It opposes the apartheid logic of black and white. As Richard Kearney writes:

> ...*the poetical imagination usually allows us to identify with the forgotten or discarded persons of our history. It invites excluded middles back into the fold, opens the door to prodigal sons and daughters, and refuses the condescending tolerance of the elite toward the preterite, the saved toward the damned.*[20]

Our notorious 'She'll be right' may be our way of groping for this more spacious kind of expression. Perhaps this is the good side of our sport and even gambling... The darker possibility also remains. It may simply mean that we tolerate our spiritual deficiencies because really there is fundamentally nothing worth exploring. Whatever the case, the first and most effective step in the right direction is to begin 'to imagine the world as it could be otherwise'.[21]

A New Search for Wisdom

Whether we are particularly religious or not, I find myself surmising that our primary need is for a 'philosophy' in the original meaning of the word, 'a love of wisdom'. I would think it is one of the main contributions the Judaeo-Christian religious community should be aiming to make. The definition of wisdom among the classic writers turned on 'knowing reality in its deepest explanation', in 'its first cause'. It looks beyond the quantifiable to the quality of life; beyond the pragmatic to the truly freeing; beyond the economy to the ecology of human life; beyond the production of images to a true poetry of the real; beyond the angry mask to the suffering face. As I said previously, Australians are positioned in a space, geographical and historical, where it is possible to take the longer and deeper view, to imagine the world otherwise.

It is not of course a simple minded, uncritical matter. It has to integrate the contribution of the great 'masters of suspicion' who have dominated the recent cultural past of Europe.[22] For instance, Marx posed a deep challenge to the religious and philosophical foundations of capitalism. After him, any faith that is unrelated to the dispossessed of one's world, is inherently suspect. As has often been pointed out, Marx's questioning of God makes Christians expose themselves to the 'dangerous memory' of Jesus who was executed as a criminal for his solidarity with the poor and the outcast in the society of that time. Christians have to imagine religious meanings in a more social manner. They now need to appropriate their faith as a way of social involvement rather than as a transcendent form of social security.

Similarly, there is the challenge of Freud. In his delving into the inarticulate and unexpressed emotional life of his patients, he concluded that religion was the projection of the immature. It was a neurotic refusal in the face of the stark business of being a self-determining human being. The religious were essentially infantile. They displaced their responsibility into a myth of the 'good Daddy', God as the ultimate 'father image'. Any religious tradition must show it is able to live with this critique and retain this suspicion about itself: is the whole panoply of religious life, the usual domain of the spiritual existence, a refuge for the infantile and immature, for those refusing the harsh realism of life and death? The Freudian movement is now established as a profession, even an industry. It exhibits its own limitations, too: therapists 'free' their clients to conform to diseased and inhuman cultural forms in which more than sexuality is repressed! But the question has been posed, and it is unwise for anyone concerned with the spiritual in our culture to deny its challenge. By freeing religious faith from infantile fantasy, the Freudian critique can release the creative potential of religious imagination.

Once more, a new imagining of religious commitment is the issue. It has to deal not with the ideology of the Sunday school or the maintenance of Catholic education, but with the faith of adults as it inspires adult freedom and respects adult conscience, as it frees the repressed spirit of our 'kidult' culture.

Then, and perhaps most importantly for the beginnings of Australian literary culture, there is Nietzsche. His name has been rendered ambiguous by the Nazi use of his myth of the 'superman'. Certainly, he is not well known to most Australians. Yet, as Tom Inglis Moore's researches indicate,[23] the Australian literary tradition owes quite a lot to this most passionate of modern philosophers. Nietzsche's rage was especially directed against the religious divinisation of the anti-human. He discerned in bourgeois Christian culture a propensity to exalt passivity, and self-abnegation, and a generally mean-spirited suspicion of the human in the name of religion. In his view, not only was Christianity a servile kind of faith, but God 'had degenerated into the contradiction of life, instead of being its transfiguration and eternal Yes! God as the declaration of war against life, against nature, against the will to live! God—the formula for every slander against "this world", for every lie about the "beyond", God the deification of nothingness, the will to nothingness pronounced holy!'[24]

It is not difficult to find in oneself a sympathetic response to what Nietzsche was getting at. The wowserism, censorious moralising, the prevalent single-issue moralities, the surprise that any religious person can be a 'good sport', all attest to the point that the passionate Teuton has made. But of course, neither then nor now, is that the whole story. Nietzsche could hardly have foreseen the time when the champions of 'transcendent humanism' would be popes, that the main protesters on behalf of a more human and just way of life would be activist Christians in the progressively monodimensional and fragmented world that has come into being. Yet he made his point; and that point remains as a challenge. It particularly resonates in Australian consciousness in its disillusionment with post-Enlightenment Christianity. To the degree that faith imagines reality in a way that looks its suffering neighbour in the eye and seizes on its own ability to promote a genuine humanity, to the degree that it is a healthy irony on all the obsessions of consumerism, it will be an essential force.

Cosmic 'Knocking'?

To integrate these challenges from the masters of suspicion into the Australian suspicion of religion, and yet to maintain a spirituality uncowed by them, is the biggest challenge of all. In Australia, the freeing of faith from its false or defective forms is often delayed by the persistence of an old-style 'scientific humanism' still flourishing in Australian universities and amongst influential journalists. The situation has gone comparatively unchallenged as generations of students graduating from church schools have been at the mercy of an untroubled, secularist educational establishment. For the university scene has, until comparatively recently, been deprived of the presence of vigorous theological faculties. Despite the availability of state recognised degrees in theology, there are no education dollars available for theological faculties, nor for the students who study within them. In this respect, Australian universities are in notable contrast to Oxford or Munich, Paris or Yale, Edinburgh or Toronto.

Then, to take another example, the well-known phrase-maker of Australian journalism, Philip Adams, brought out his *Adams versus God*.[25] The cover, in an obvious parody of Michelangelo's 'Creation', depicts a smugly reclining fig-leafed Phil tweaking the finger of a rather startled deity. No local Ayatollah called for his chastisement on religious or cultural grounds! Apart from being a good example of Aussie-style 'knocking', in this case taken to cosmic proportions, the book strangely mixes agnostic fundamentalism with wonder at the proportions of the universe and the mystery of human life within it: '...stop bloody well complaining about things and consider for a moment the astonishment of being alive in an endless Luna Park of atoms and galaxies, in a world where you can laugh, listen to music, eat, make love and children. And make a fool of yourself.'[26] While Adams is mightily impressed with the achievement of science, theology is 'merely fiction masquerading as scholarship'; it legitimates harsh and conservative emotions; it is inadequate in explaining the cosmos, and so on. Of course, Adams selectively drops any reference to the religious dimension in the review from which he draws his scientific data. The author of this review refers to the 'unanswerable, super-ultimate question, why is there something rather than nothing?', and goes on to quote Chesterton about 'the universe being the most exquisite masterpiece ever constructed by nobody'.[27] Adams would be wary of the concerns of the noted biologist, the late Sir Alister Hardy, who set up a Religious Experience Research Unit at Manchester College, Oxford. Perhaps, in Philip Adam's documented capacity for wonder, compassion and even for fun, the learned scientist might have found evidence of 'religious experiences'! Then, too, as we look at the struggles for justice in Australia and beyond, what would Adams make of Murray's judgment that 'It is generations since being an agnostic involved any daring, and atheism tends to put one into coercive rather than generous company'.[28]

New Questions, Fresh Opportunities

The Australian mind in some of its educational and cultural manifestations does not seem to have realised how 'narrowspeak' science has engineered so much destruction at the price of progress. Such scientism, to give it its more accurate name, is characterised by a truncated, flat view of reality as mere quantifiable and manipulable matter. It chooses to ignore the wider deeper range of human values. The influential American Passionist visionary, Tom Berry, catches the dimensions of the problem we are struggling with, as he refers to the history of the last two hundred years of Western thought:

> *During this period the human mind lived in the narrowest bonds it has ever experienced. The vast mythic, visionary, symbolic world with its all-pervasive numinous qualities was lost. Because of this*

> loss, humanity made its terrifying assault upon the earth with an
> irrationality that is stunning in enormity while we were being
> assured that this was the way to a better, more humane, more
> reasonable world.[29]

Unwittingly it has cramped human freedoms into the con-
straints of big government and mass control. It has irreversibly
damaged the environment. Now the purely scientific mind is
recognised to be as alien to human reality as the most fun-
damentalist bigotry. Having no values of its own, it was and
remains up for sale to the highest bidder—those forces whether
commercial, national or multi-national, which will let it get on
with its job without asking the uncomfortable human questions. Over one half of the world's scientists are involved in
arms production and weapons research. With an eye to our
particular context, Stephen Graubard poses a searching question:

> Whether Australians today possess the self-esteem and self-aware-
> ness to raise such questions and to relate them to larger issues
> dealing with the complex problems of national security in a world
> of atomic arms, is to ask whether they are still capable of drawing
> on their much-discussed powers of political ingenuity and inven-
> tiveness and whether their isolation still provides certain intellec-
> tual advantages. The Australian experience raises profound
> questions about the reality and meaning of national independence
> in the world today, but also about the continuing hazards of
> provincialism—not to speak of the unacknowledged power and
> influence of a recent colonial subordination.[30]

The open, spacious mind trying to enter into a 'wholespeak'
conversation is, in no small way, stimulated by genuine science
itself. Increasingly we are confronted with a universe of all but
incredible mystery. In the words of one reputable scientist, we
are dealing with 'a universe proving to be not only more
mysterious than we can imagine but even more mysterious
than we could imagine' (J.B.Haldane). The former scientific
myth of a scientist dispassionately analysing the world down
to its smallest 'building blocks' is all but abandoned. Such an
atomisation of reality has yielded to new sciences of complexity, with their emphasis on the inter-related network of the
whole. Now the leading metaphor is the hologram—not the
isolated particle nor the one-dimensional analysis. What is
emerging in the global intellectual scene is clear enough to

perceive. It is a rejection of the 'nothing but' approach of a flat monodimensional exploration of reality. The mind of the artist, the scientist, the mystic, the philosopher are not so much interpretations of the universe of our existence, but qualitative dimensions of it. It is a universe coming to itself as known, as loved, as reverenced, as inviting humanity to relate to its creative unfolding. If the 'narrowspeak' of science once could rule out the 'wholespeak' of the big questions, today's leading scientists are those most searching for a more comprehensive view.[31]

Richard Allen captures the exhausted spirit of this limited side of the 'first Enlightenment' in his evocative little poem, 'Epitaph for the Western Intelligentsia':[32]

what we come round to
in the end
is that all our thinking
has brought us nowhere

that the trail-blazing journey
has ended where it began
that thought at best
is a protection against further thought

that the heathens we sought to save
the masses to educate
need neither our salvation
nor our education

that we therefore
serve no particular purpose
perform no particular function
have no particular place to go

& we roll to the ground
& we cry out like children
& we bark like dogs
& we learn to wag our tails.

The Second Enlightenment

All this points to the need for a 'second Enlightenment'. Australia was a unique creation of the first Enlightenment. It was all but completely cut off from any deeply nurturing tradition of larger intelligence. The 'first Enlightenment' was a radical, critical break from any subservience of intelligence to what was apprehended as an extrinsic authority, be it church, state or the classical philosophical traditions of the West. Its heroic myth in terms of intelligence was that of the individual critic throwing off the shackles of the received wisdom. In terms of economics, it was that of the individual entrepreneur developing the resources of the industrial revolution in a government-endorsed *laissez-faire*. Religiously, it was at best tolerantly relativist. While it could examine the symbols and products of religions to pass judgments on them without any sense of their real poetry and disclosive power, it saw genuine knowledge only in the domain of empirical science. Its greatest success was 'science' in the empirical domain of the measurable and physically quantifiable. What could not be measured and managed could hardly be said to exist.

Today from many perspectives, this first Enlightenment has run its course, and the need for new models, new apprehensions of the real, is being felt. The price to pay for the dominance of science was reduction of everything to quantifiable terms. It took time to become not only critically intelligent, but intelligently imaginative in a more comprehensively human sense. For human existence was not merely a physical, higher animal existence, but one nourished on values. Darwin may have put us into the on-going process of biological evolution, but our continuance in such a genesis has become now a matter of choices and freedom. Freud may have unmasked the realms of the 'unconscious', but there was also an unconscious, a 'superconscious', of transcendence and spirit. Marx may have outlined the dialectic materialism of history in economic terms, but there was a drama and tragedy of human existence of which he would not dream. Nietzsche discerned the anti-human in religion, but failed to see the day when religion would be the force most concerned with human values in a technologically flattened world.

And in many domains of the physical and human sciences this second Enlightenment is taking place. The new sciences of complexity point to the limits of 'particle analysis' in their attempt to suggest more holistic models of reality. Fritjof Capra suggests in his *The Turning Point. Science, Society and the Rising Culture* that the new model of reality is the hologram, as I have already mentioned.[33] In contrast to the two-dimensional representation of the chart, the sign, or the standard photography, this new technique of lensless photography gives a multidimen-

79

sional view of the object. It symbolises a more holistic vision of reality. The emergence of this is evident in many ways. In modern physics, as I have mentioned, the search for grand unified theory yields such exciting modern paradigms as implicate order and the bootstrap theory. Ecological consciousness, and its attendant sciences, is another manifestation. Modern studies of the human mind, not uninfluenced by Jung, and recent appreciation of 'right brain' activity, are attending to the more complex phenomenon of human consciousness and its role in the exploration of reality. Our consciousness does not find its exclusive model in the reactions of the laboratory rat, nor in the pathology of the diseased mind, but in the consciousness of healthy, self-transcending, imaginative human beings flourishing in a whole environment of cosmic, cultural, social and historical proportions. Sociologically, theorists such as Tallcot, Parsons, Berger and Bellah, and Michael Mason here in Australia, have worked toward a more comprehensive sociology. In contrast to the sociological methods of the preceding era, the emerging sociology is far more hospitable to transcendent concerns and values. Culturally speaking, probably the most vivid indication of this new holistic vision of reality is the feminist critique of the modern culture. Though this is a varied and often confusing phenomenon, its central point can hardly be gainsaid: reality has been too long affirmed and explored in exclusively 'male' terms, by masculine agents, for masculine ends. It calls for a new understanding of history, politics, morality, religion and society, in the light of feminine experience and insight.

A distinctively Australian emblem of this second enlightenment is found in our growing appreciation of the depths of Aboriginal culture. As Eugene Stockton writes:

In the harshest continent on earth, they learnt to survive by entering into partnership with the land which became a whole way of life, a spirituality. Spiritual development was preferred to the technological in satisfying the basic needs and higher aspirations of a society, moulded as it was like no other and over a greater stretch of time in the matrix of a mothering land.[34]

Education Again

All this is raising profound questions for the very meaning of education. That education is meant to equip the rising generation to deal with the 'real world' is hardly a matter of dispute. What that real world is, of course, is the radical question. In times of economic crisis, the temptation is to see it merely in terms of marketable skills. Yet at the same time it is the youth who keep seeing reality as more than that. And it is they, be it through the hazards of unemployment, or disillusionment with a materialist view of life, who most evidence a rejection of such pragmatism. For some of them, the only way in which to escape into what is imagined to be a more liberated world, is through the use of narcotic drugs. And in that we have a tragedy of immense proportions, leaving society debating strategies for facing it. The economic crisis is both the cause and effect of the much deeper problem of a society struggling to find fresh bearings.

What, then, is education? Surely it means formation in the fundamental skills, meanings and values of the culture (including economic and technological skills). But it is also about transformation, the awakening to wisdom and freedom which cannot be so neatly programmed. It includes vision and responsibility and a holistic sense of the universe. Surely this too is within the scope of any concerned educational enterprise. As I said earlier, the aim of education is the question aching beneath all our plans for the future: is it intent on promoting the emergence of a truly personal society in which the great meanings and values are taken seriously? Or, is it content to programme a workforce which will have to look for its real education elsewhere?

I might note in passing that even the great Swiss educational psychologist, Piaget, so influential in educational theory, was all but exclusively interested in the developing capacities for rational thought in the young. The place of art, of religious faith, of other areas of human perception, were little recognised. This limitation of intelligence to the rational and the abstract must now be corrected in a larger respect for the varied capacities of human intelligence to explore reality.[35] This will necessarily have profound consequences in educational theory and practice. For the wholeness of human imagination, having undergone a severe mutilation, is now re-asserting its health and wanting something more.

Spiritual Liberation

Set in this context, spirituality becomes an urgent issue. Bernard Lonergan, one of the seminal influences in the analysis of human consciousness,[36] crystallises our capacities for soul-nourishing and progress-promoting truth in his axiom: 'genuine objectivity is the fruit of authentic subjectivity'.[37] Our only way to the real is by consenting to the manifold dynamics of human consciousness itself. These include our capacities to attend to and to be open to the whole range of data offered in human experience; our abilities to question the meaning of such data by posing all the relevant questions; our creativity in imagining the possible real and the refinement of our sensibilities in feeling for it; our willingness to accept the evidence; our readiness to ask what could or should be the case; the distinctively human challenge of responsibility in light of the reasons and values disclosed. Finally, to set all this within a horizon which resists any form of arbitrary limitation. There the human person is drawn into a transcendent realm of the meaning of all our meanings, the sufficient reason for all our sufficient reasons, the worthwhileness of all our decisions and values. Our reaching out to the ultimate and the absolute is not some religious caprice, nor the projection of human insecurity, but a profound consent to the dynamism of human consciousness itself. Let me quote Lonergan more fully:

> *The question of God, then, lies within man's horizon. Man's transcendental subjectivity is mutilated or abolished, unless he is stretching forth toward the intelligible, the unconditioned, the good of value. The reach not of his attainment but of his intending is unrestricted. There lies within his horizon a region for the divine, a shrine of ultimate holiness. It cannot be ignored. The atheist may pronounce it empty. The agnostic may say that he has found his investigation inconclusive. The contemporary humanist will refuse to allow the question to arise. But these negations presuppose the spark in our clod, our native orientation to the divine.[38]*

We have been pondering on the extent to which this 'transcendental subjectivity' is 'mutilated or abolished' in the context of Australian culture. The 'narrowspeak' of the atheist, the agnostic, the humanist and, perhaps most damagingly, the religious, has had its say. But, in these different ways, it is capable of drowning out the 'wholespeak' that would point to the 'shrine of ultimate holiness' within human consciousness. The spiritual integrity of our consciousness, of soul and imagination, is radically frustrated when it is has no space in which to expand. Hence a fundamental question: To what degree is the main thrust of our educational system, in its present form, a systematic foreclosure on the spiritual?

Yet it is in a thoroughly intelligent context that this issue of spirituality arises. It can claim to be an essential part of the 'education issue'. For spirituality is concerned with promoting the 'integrity', the authentic subjectivity of the human person in his or her deepest relationships with the 'other'. It is inherently concerned for the deepest feelings of solidarity with those for whom our present utopia is really no place at all. It insists on the courage to face ultimate questions, and to surrender to absolute values. And it seeks to foster a critical imaginative appropriation of ultimate answers in the measure that they are still available in the struggling religious traditions of our culture.

'Wholespeak' and Poetic Imagination

Modern consciousness is nourished by a world of expanding knowledge including everything from quarks to quasars, everything from alpha waves to black holes, from DNA to supernovas. Within human consciousness the universe comes to itself in a unique way. It becomes luminous to itself in the human awareness which billions of years of biogenesis has brought forth. In the human mind, it awakes to the 'whole' as origin and destiny, as the ultimate horizon of our present life. Australian poetry, as Les Murray's *Anthology of Australian Religious Poetry* indicates, has plenty of instances of the experiences of the 'whole' and of the 'wholespeak' which evokes it. Let me give a couple of examples.

James McAuley in his 'Credo' pivots between intelligent wonder at the uncanny givenness of complex reality and its occurrence within human consciousness:

That each thing is a word
Requiring us to speak it:
from the ant to the quasar,
from the clouds to the ocean floor–

> *The meaning not ours, but found*
> *in the mind deeply submissive*
> *to the grammar of existence,*
> *The syntax of the real.*[39]

Spirituality is this deep submission of the mind in the face of the mystery of the real. Far from being a preciously defended inward, individual 'enclosed garden', the human spirit is only at home when it is receptive to a universe of incredible diversity: 'the meaning not ours...' In this fundamental interaction, human art, intelligence and faith transmute the mere brute givenness of reality ('the world's bare tokens') into a sense of transcendent mystery: the alien becomes the domain of the human, the thing begins to dwell in human consciousness as 'thought'; the physical becomes the sacramental symbol of the ultimate:

> *So that alien is changed*
> *to human, thing into thinking:*
> *For the world's bare tokens*
> *we pay golden coin*
> *Stamped with the king's image;*
> *And poems are prophecy*
> *Of a new heaven and a new earth,*
> *A rumour of resurrection.*

This sense of human indwelling in the mystery of the universe is not unlike Heidegger's notion of primal thinking. Rather than being in the first instance detached, technical analysis, thinking is first of all akin to 'thanking'. It lives as an openness receptive to the uncanny whole.[40] Such a thanking kind of thinking makes for the spiritual space in which true reflection can occur. Any thinking confined to the one-dimensional technological level cannot but be the forgetfulness of what is most meaningful and essential to the soul. Such flat thinking is inherently closed to philosophic wonder. Spiritual traditions have called this kind of holistic thinking contemplation or meditation. It is the quiet activity of mind receptive to the whole: the mind is liberated to allow the universe to occur as a wonder, in the uncanny mystery of what it is.

As further examples, let me refer to two poems by Judith Wright. Without putting too tight a pattern on poetry, we can read them as an invitation to a deeper wisdom and a larger sense of the wholeness of reality. The first, 'The Forest' invites to a sense of mystery, the ultimate dimensions of truth, which, however unspoken, is the ground out of which all our finite meanings grow. The poet is reflecting on a life of exploration with its careful catalogue of experiences as it names each plant and flower in its different seasons. It seemed to offer an endless scope of exploration. It offered an intoxicating fullness of information: 'time's renewing harvest/ could never reach an end'. But then comes another season of deeper questioning, of going beyond the variations and the variety to something more. The pertinent verses are as follows:

> *Now that its vines and flowers*
> *are named and known,*
> *like long fulfilled desires,*
> *those first strange joys are gone.* [41]

It is as though we are being introduced to one typical 'first Enlightenment' experience with the eventual disappearance of the 'first strange joys'. It leads to a concern for the ultimate, the transcendent, the permanent:

> *My search is further.*
> *There's still to name and know*
> *beyond the flowers I gather*
> *that one that will not wither—*
> *the truth from which they grow.*

The paradise of simple innocent self-confident knowledge knocks on the door of philosophy, the love of wisdom: 'my search is further…the truth that makes them grow'. This is the intellectual component of spirituality, living in the presence of mystery that still has to be named and known.

The same poet in 'Five Senses' suggests a more inward experience of such truth in human consciousness. Consciousness itself resonates in a strange correlation with reality, a reciprocal indwelling of each in the other. A deeper mystery of the self is disclosed. It gathers reality into consciousness to experience what is at once dark and light, still and moving, a dance and a design. Personal consciousness far from being lost in a plethora of objects is the nodal point at which reality concentrates and comes home:

> *Now my five senses*
> *gather into meaning*
> *all acts, all presences;*

> *and as a lily gathers*
> *the elements together,*
> *in me this dark and shining,*
> *that stillness and that moving,*
> *these shapes that spring from nothing,*
> *become a rhythm that dances,*
> *a pure design.*[42]

This apparently subjective concentration opens into a self-transcendence. The concentrated inwardness expands into a sense of receptivity to something other. Reality is experienced in the self as being beholden to some transcendent other, 'the weaver', and to some universal belonging in an uncanny pattern and rhythm that 'is not mine'.

> *While I'm in my five senses*
> *they send me spinning*
> *all sounds and silences,*
> *all shape and colour*
> *as threads from the weaver*
> *whose web within me growing*
> *follows beyond my knowing*
> *some patterns sprung from nothing-*
> *a rhythm that dances*
> *and is not mine.*

Such exercises of Australian poetic imagination are remarkable evocations of the 'whole self' as it awakens in human experience. They suggest how mind and soul are ultimately nourished by what is transcendent and absolute. Natively the human self is participating in mystery. Our deepest consciousness discloses this in its awareness of the pattern 'sprung from nothing', 'beyond my knowing', the dance of the ultimate reality in the human mind.

Spirituality, in this context, is essentially intelligence alive to the wonder and mystery which cannot be suppressed without mutilating the deepest sense of self. It frees consciousness from the superficial, the absurd, the tragically alienated, into a sense of the dynamic interrelated whole. The poems I have cited evidence a resistance to the closing of the Australian mind, even as they inspire a new openness.

Religious faith, of course, ideally subsumes such basic human experiences. The tragedy in Australian culture is that it does not. Too often, it appears as a moralistic and unintelligent code which promises to save souls but does not nourish them.

A faith without a philosophy, without an imagination, cannot collaborate in the more general search for wisdom in Australian culture. In the measure that it learns new ways to think and imagine, its millennial wisdom, along with its sacraments and parables of life, will re-emerge when they are most needed.

---

1. From *Discourse on Thinking* by Martin Heidegger, translated by John M. Anerson and E. Hans Freund. English language translation © 1966 by Harper & Row, Publishers, Inc. Reprinted with permission of the publisher.

2. Patrick White, 'A Sense of Integrity', *Arena* 84, 1988, p. 98.

3. See Leonie Kramer, 'The Media, Society and Culture', *Australia...*, pp. 294–295.

4. Kramer, p. 305.

5. For an incisive, conservative view of the matter, see Lauchlan Chipman, 'The Children of Cynicism', in *The New Conservatism in Australia*, (Robert Mann, ed.), Oxford University Press, Melbourne, 1982, pp. 17–39. This varied collection of essays makes one wonder whether 'thinking' always appears 'conservative' in Australia!
    For more economically concerned remarks, see Peter Ellyard, the present Director of the Commission for the Future, 'Desirable Futures for Australia', In *Future* 12, April, 1989, p. 8.

    > *Present day Australia still tends to have a 'third-world' view that wealth comes from beneath the ground, or 'off the hoof', rather than between the ears. If we are to develop a 'brain-base' economy in Australia, we will need to use much more effectively the contribution of...creative people.*

6. Simon and Schuster, New York, 1987.

7. For a related and incisive treatment see Theodore Rosznak, *The Cult of Information. The Folklore of Computers and the True Art of Thinking*, Pantheon, New York, 1986, especially chapters 5 and 10.

8. Graham English's insightful reappraisal of religious education confirms and stimulates my own approach: 'Imagination: the Past and Future of Religious Education', *Word in Life*, 1989, pp. 9–11.

9. The philosopher Richard Campbell makes a number of valuable points in his article, 'The Philosophical Environment of Theologising in Australia', R. Wittycombe (ed.), *Australian and New Zealand Religious History*, ANZTS/ATS, Canberra, pp. 33–43.

10. Paul Ricoeur, *Freud and Philosophy: An Essay on Interpretation*, trans. Denis Savage, Yale University Press, New Haven, 1970, p. 543.

11. Tom Inglis Moore, *Social Patterns in Australian Literature*, Angus and Robertson, Sydney, 1971.

12. See Daniel Boorstin, *The Guide to Pseudo Events in America*, Random House, New York, 1971.

13. 'The Gravy of Images', *Compass Theology Review* 23, Summer 1988, pp. 21–28.

14. Robert Hughes, *The Shock of the New*, BBC publications, London, p. 387.

15. Caroline Jones' interviews over the last few years on the ABC have been a conspicuous and heartening exception. For a statement of her approach, together with some instances, see her book, *The Search for Meaning* Melbourne: ABC with Collins Dove, 1989.

16. See Les Murray's poem, 'The Vol sprung from Heraldry': 'Left wing, right wing:/ two wings torment our lives,/two wings without a body,/joined, turkey wing and vulture wing...'

17. Richard Kearney, *The Wake of the Imagination*, p. 367.

18. Donald Horne, 'Who Rules Australia?', *Australia...*, pp. 171–195. Note, too, my previous remarks on David O'Reilly 'The Hatred Factor' *Intelligencer*, May, 1989, pp. 1–5 (see Ch.3, endnote 44).

19. Hugh Collins 'Political Ideology in Australia', *Australia...*, p. 154.

20. Kearney, p. 369.

21. Kearney, p. 371.

22. A useful resource here is Hans Küng, *Does God Exist?*, Random House, New York, 1981.

23. Moore, pp. 252–7. Interestingly, neither Marx nor Freud rate a mention in this rather comprehensive survey.

24. *The Portable Nietzsche*, (Walter Kaufmann, ed.), The Viking Press, New York, 1968, pp. 585–586.

25. Nelson, Melbourne, 1985.

26. Adams, p. 191. See my review in *The New Catholic Worker*, Jan.–Feb., 1986, pp. 4–5.

27. Martin Gardner in the *New York Review of Books*, 13 June, 1985, pp. 31–34.

28. Les Murray, *Embodiment and Incarnation*, Aquinas Library, Brisbane, 1987, p. 10.

29. 'The New Story: Comments on the Origin, Identification and Transmission of Values'. *Cross Currents*, Summer/Fall, 1987, pp. 198–200.

30. *Australia...*, pp.x–xi.

31. See the insightful study by a leading Australian philosopher, John Honner, *The Description of Nature: Niels Bohr and the Philosophy of Quantum Physics*, Clarendon Press, Oxford, 1987.

32. *Anthology...*, p. 123.

33. Fontana, London, 1984.

34. Eugene Stockton, 'The Blackened Stump is Holy Seed', *Compass Theology Review* 22, Autumn-Winter 1988, p. 21.

35. See David Helminiak, *Spiritual Development: An Interdisciplinary Study*, Loyola University Press, Chicago, 1987.

36. For the broader context, see Eugene Webb, *Philosophers of Consciousness*, University of Washington Press, Washington, 1987. This excellent exposition deals with the thought of Polanyi, Lonergan, Voegelin, Ricoeur, Girard and Kierkegaard.

37. *Method...*, p. 292.

38. *Method...*, p. 103. For further applications of Lonergan's work to spirituality see John Bathersby, *The Foundations of Christian Spirituality in Bernard Lonergan, SJ,* N. Pecheuz, Rome, 1982; and the regrettably unpublished dissertation of Frank Fletcher, *Exploring Christian Theology's Foundations in Religious Experience*, Melbourne College of Divinity, 1982.

39. *Anthology...*, p. 180. Reprinted from *Collected Poems 1930–70,* © Norma Mc Auley, 1971, by permission of Angus & Robertson Publishers/Collins.

40. Most accessibly in *Discourse on Thinking*.

41. *Anthology...*, p. 221. Reprinted from *Collected Poems 1942–70,* © Judith Wright, 1971, by permission of Angus & Robertson Publishers/Collins.

42. *Anthology...*, p. 221. Reprinted from *Collected Poems 1942–70,* © Judith Wright, 1971, by permission of Angus & Robertson Publishers/Collins.

Chapter 5:
Imagining Our Past:
Our Story

'The moment a society wishes to give an official story of itself, it becomes a lie. This is exactly what has happened in the year of the Bicentenary- which is also the year of the great Australian lie. Not that it hasn't had its positive, stimulating moments- the arrival of the ships in Sydney Harbour for instance, when for a few hours Australians seemed to forget their squabbles and to become more or less reconciled to one another. This already seems a long time ago. Since then we have been all out for the jugular in one another's throats. Perhaps it is normal in a jungle where the human beast is the most savage of all—where for all our rationalising and material progress, we more or less take it for granted that our behaviour shall be sustained by lies.' (Patrick White)[1]

As I noted in Chapter 3, the American sociologist, Robert Bellah, wrote, 'No one has changed a great nation without appealing to its soul'.[2] The 'soul' in question here, so elusive and inarticulate in Australia, is the awareness of the great poem within us of which Les Murray spoke. We could take this a step further. This poem, it seems to me, is the residue of the stories that we have judged worth telling, the stories by which we express who we are, where we came from, and where we go from here. If it is not to neglect the challenge of the present, conscience needs to imagine its past.

The Real Story

Bicentenary Australia has invited a retelling of the Australian story. It has made us all think of how such a short story is to be told within the larger narrative of Aboriginal Australia. Multicultural concerns and commitments provoke questions about how an extraordinary variety of national stories can be heard in such a way as to nourish the identity of modern Australians in our continent of experience. How is our modern success story open to the stories of pain, isolation and defeat that characterised our past? How do all such aspects of our story come together into a hopeful retelling of who we are, and what we want to become?[3]

On the individual level amnesia is never particularly productive. To forget one's story is to lose one's self and the basic direction of existence. So too in the larger context. Symbols from our past, be they treasured or dreaded—Botany Bay, the Irish story, Norfolk Island, Port Arthur and Moreton Bay, the Gold Rush, the ill-fated explorations into the interior, Gallipoli, sporting legends such as the 'Bodyline series'—are all part of it. They have often been set into the simple form of taking a risk and being courageous in defeat. Real history has become a moral tale. The issue seems to be one of being open to the whole story. The unexamined past can be a dead weight if it is not imaginatively retrieved and owned, in all its forgotten promise and pain. If we are not to stick into a congealed version of our history, the mix of the official story must be kept stirred by a keener, sharper recollection of suffering. The success story, defensive of its achievements and its heroes, has to undergo a more compassionate retelling. What was disowned must now be included. Those who apparently failed or were defeated, who had no story worth the telling, must now be given time if our history is to be more than a national ideology. One great story teller, Patrick White, makes this point. He writes:

> *A nation in the true sense isn't born of self-congratulation and the accumulation of often ill-gotten and unequally distributed wealth. I suppose I'll be condemned as a miserable Jeremiah if I say it is born of suffering. Australians have suffered in the past, which they tend to forget now that they're on with the bonfires, the champagne (the ad-man's magic lure) and the festivals...[4]*

As Manning Clark recently reminded us, and incidently gives a useful key to his own vast historical work, 'Every generation writes its own history in its own image: every generation admits into the portals of the heroes men fashioned in their own image.. One generation, we are told cometh, and another passeth: the earth abideth forever.'[5] In his biblical allusiveness, he goes on to suggest that the earth itself is the only hero that Australians, black and white, have come to accept. He sees the current effort to write the real history of Australia as being a quest for other heroes as well. Such will relativise the established heroes as representing only a truncated version of ourselves:

> Some of the fathers of the new generation have already taken their seats on the penitents stools. The children have burrowed around in the past to find heroes who are pleasing in their sight. The men who wanted to have life and to have it more abundantly, the men who wanted to make amends for male domination in Australia have been up for examination as potential heroes. Aborigines who resisted the white man's domination have already appeared in the history books...[6]

The Untold Story

Our whole story is of course made up of millions of stories, stories in which brutality and degradation combine with freedom and a wonderful expanding sense of the new and the fresh start; stories of isolation and discovery, of heroic sacrifice and the most repulsive greed; stories of lawlessness and strange law-abidingness; stories of England and Ireland, now linked with the dozens of other national stories. When we try to tell our stories, or to hear them anew, our imagination is always in crisis; it is never finished; neither others nor ourselves can be reduced to an image. The compassionate story enlarges conscience. It invites us to join with real people, companions into a future which is the only thing we have in common. So I would like to refer to a few special stories here. They may serve to keep the imagination alive and enlarge the sense of our shared humanity.

Australia is a largely forgotten story in the world of modern myths. It has been a little Cinderella story of survival in half oblivion. Hardly worth the telling in the great history of the world, but a subversive story for all that:

> *If America, then France and the other countries which followed her revolt against feudal hierarchy, are the bourgeois revolution, Australia is perhaps the proletarian evolution, and what develops from that fact may be more productive for mankind than what develops from the effort to suppress or disguise it. We began as the poor who were sent away to England's South Sea Gulag, and our continent was largely settled by the poor who got away...* [7]

In the modern world of myths of progress and success, the Australian story occurs as a parable upsetting what was so grandly set up: here, on the underside of history, in the remote and isolated Down Under, a parable is told subverting the grand stories of parent Britain. Here, what was thought to matter was revealed as not mattering at all; and the serious things of 'over there' were laughed at down here. Here, the despised, the condemned and the forgotten possessed the land.

A Fortunate Life?

You might hear this story in Bert Facey's *A Fortunate Life*. [8] Even the title is a parable, for it is a story of incredible suffering: a parentless boy, eight years old, starting to work in the outback of Western Australia, travelled from place to place to experience both cruelty and tenderness. Almost murdered by the stockwhip of a drink-crazed farm-hand, he grows up to face death and wounding in the dreadful experience of Gallipoli. There he suffers the loss of his brother and friends. He returns to lose his farm in the depression, and to lose his own son in the Second World War. Finally, he is left bereft of his loving wife after sixty years. A fortunate life? How ironic, and more so when he makes a confused statement of his lack of belief in God. [9] Any notion of God was lost in the violence of the bayonet charge, in religion's capacity to prey on a person's conscience, in the hatreds and divisiveness religion has caused, in the scandal of religious ownership of enormous wealth while people are starving. He permits himself quite an outburst: 'No sir, there is no God, it is only a myth.'

And yet the parable. Jan Carter, in her perceptive little 'Afterword', makes two interesting remarks on Facey's apparent lack of religion.[10] In likening his book to an Australian *Pilgrim's Progress*, she points out that an extraordinary sense of Providence brought this pilgrim of humanity through danger and despair. She implies, too, that he felt himself linked to those he loved, in all the fidelities of life and even beyond death. On the testimony of his daughter, he would go off to the cemetery to sit and think by his beloved wife's grave. 'Going off, as he said, to have a talk with my darling'.[11] Indeed, he says he had two lives, before marriage and after: 'Before I married I was on my own. It was a lonely solitary life—Evelyn changed that. After our marriage my life became something which was much more than just me.' You wonder if there were not three lives, the third being the final years after his wife's death when he repossessed the whole story of his life in thankfulness and hope. Whatever the case, we have in Bert's 'fortunate life' a document of what any believer would aspire to in the practice of hope and charity. The ultimate, though largely unspoken, is lived. This 'fortunate life' suggests itself as a parable of a 'fortunate history'. It invites modern Australians to look back with Bert into the sufferings and mystery that have gone into our making. Somewhere, there, the grace of a new beginning lies hidden and waiting.

A Courageous Life

Then there is another story which I pluck out of Robert Hughes' magnificent, *The Fatal Shore*.[12] He returns quite often in his pages to the exploits of an Irish convict, a certain Lawrence Frayne, who through unbelievable torture on Norfolk Island lived to tell the tale. It is an account of astonishing survival, of rebellion against all the odds embodied in the brutalising system that was Norfolk Island and those who administered it. Frayne seemed to grasp that human dignity was at stake. Repeatedly flogged already, he is brought clanking in his chains before the monstrous Morriset, governor of the Island prison, for breaking a flagstone in a quarry ('as usual I found my defence useless'). He is sentenced to a hundred lashes: 'After the sentence I plainly told the Commandant that he was a tyrant. He replied that no one had said that about him before.

I said they knew the consequences too well to tell him so. But I tell you in stark naked blunt English that you are as great a tyrant as Nero ever was.' The moment he spoke these words he was sentenced to an additional hundred lashes, and condemned to be kept chained down in a cell for life, never to see daylight again.

New and heavier 'cats' were procured for his punishment, and he was flayed with special cruelty. 'But I knew my innocence and bore up against it.'[13] Morriset sought new pretexts to break him. Nine weeks later Frayne is dragged into that sadistic presence, again on a trumped-up charge. Once more he stood up to his tormentor. This time he was given three hundred lashes. With his whole body scarified, all he could do was lie down on the stone floor of his solitary cell in a mixture of water and urine to relieve his pain. He is then clapped into the dumb cell, a totally dark, soundless, stone isolation chamber for two months. He staggers out half-blind, and is immediately in trouble again for consorting with some Irish female convicts: another hundred lashes. His doomed, hopeless courage led him to suffer a further three years loaded with the heaviest irons, and tied to an iron cable every night. He knew he was being singled out as an example and began to despair... 'I began to question in my own then-perverted mind the infinite mercy, nay the justice of the Deity itself.' Yet, chained there he prayed the great psalm:

> *I am counted with them that go down into the pit,*
> *I am as a man that hath no help,*
> *cast off among the dead,*
> *like the slain that lie in the grave,*
> *whom thou rememberest no more;*
> *and they are cut off from thy hand*
> *Thou has laid me in the lowest pit,*
> *in the dark places, in the deeps.*

Though tempted to suicide, he evinces an incredible religious hope and decides to keep struggling.[14] He plans further rebellion and prays for heaven's vengeance on 'this wholesale murderer and despicable white savage.' He records his revulsion against the utter inhumanity of the degrading system in which he is caught:

> *If you endeavour to take out of a prisoner that manly confidence that ought to be cherished in every civilised human being, then you*

> begin the work of demoralisation, and it will end in the very dregs
> of debasement, and an insensibility to every species of integrity and
> decency, and eradicate every right feeling in the human breast.[15]

The last glimpse we have of him in Hughes' book is when he
erects a headstone for his friend and fellow Irishman, William
Storey, who had been shot after escaping. It can be read today:
'This stone was erected by Lawrence Frayne to commemorate
his memory.' It is an emblem of what our history might be—a
headstone erected to the memory of the Lawrence Fraynes, and
the thousands who suffered such unbelievable inhumanity,
then and now, as they prayed in hope for an answer, the Jobs
of our history.

Reclaimed Lives

Then there is Sally Morgan's *My Place*. It is a moving account
of how the author, as a young woman, courageously searched
for, and, indeed, searched out, her Aboriginal roots. What had
been hidden under a couple of generations of silence was
forced to emerge as an issue to be faced, and eventually, as a
fact to be grateful for. In the book's dedication to her family,
Sally Morgan quotes a passage that also appears later in her
story:

> How deprived we would have been
> if we had been willing
> to let things stay as they were.
> We would have survived
> but not as a whole people.
> We would never have known our place.[16]

The first half of the book lets us into Sally's sense of 'things
as they were', with all the hints and evasions and troubling
questions that a bright young girl could sense. She presents
herself as a child of a troubled home: her father, a psychological
casualty of the war, with the resultant hard drinking and
growing ill health, is in and out of hospital until his tragic death
when Sally is nine years old.

Glad, her mother, is hard-pressed to make ends meet, caught
up in all the exhaustion of rearing a large family in precarious
economic circumstances. Her grandmother, 'Nan', a vigilant

and so secretive presence, educates the young girl to an intense sympathy with nature, yet keeps so much from her. Nan's suspicion of all government, her disappearances when visitors are around, her utter refusal to speak of the past, gradually posed big questions for the young detective, 'What people are we?' Were they really of Indian origin as she had been led to believe? Her suspicions eventually lead to her discovery of the 'white lie' about her family's origins. Then she decided to research the matter more deeply.

Gradually she follows up the leads—the Drake-Brockman connection, the Corunna Downs location, the appearance of Arthur, Nan's brother, 'proud of being a blackfella' with his stories and photographs, the incomplete birth certificates... Warned by her mother against causing hurt, Sally's reply is emblematic of the spirit of her journey into the past: 'Mum, it's already hurt people. It's hurt you and me and Nan, all of us. I mean, for years, I've been telling people I'm Indian! I have a right to know my own history.'

The rest of the book tells of her journey to Wollongong to hear the story of her nonagenarian Aunt Alice, and her pilgrimage back to the place of her origins with her husband, children and mother. In filling out the three stories of Uncle Arthur, her mother, and her grandmother, *My Place* becomes a document of deep emotion and home-coming. Perhaps most deeply it is a story of reconciliation: obviously for Sally herself, and her family; but something of much wider relevance. This is the reconciliation that Australia itself needs to experience as it owns the brutal racism and exploitation of its past.

A remarkable current flowing through this journal of self-discovery is a deep religious experience. Sally repeatedly expresses her own deep religious faith.[17] Arthur is a kind of Aboriginal Bert Facey, but with this difference: he frequently expresses his Christian faith in terms which are strikingly compassionate, given the environment of exploitation and racial prejudice in which he lived.[18] It seems that God was never dead for the Aboriginal people of our past, even if he were absent from the hearts of so many of their white exploiters. The lament of their history enters into our present through the words of the dying Nan: 'Do you think we'll get some respect? I'd like to think the black man will get treated the same as the white man one day. Be good, wouldn't it? By gee, it'd be good.'[19] One can easily apply to this inspiring human document the words of Manning Clark:

> *The people, not the mighty men of renown, have become the heroes of the new generation of historians. So far the people have not appeared in their books and articles as recognisable human beings. Commodities have pushed human beings off the pages of Australian history. But in time these 'new men' will probably discover the comic, the epic, the tragic figures in the history of the common people. The discerning ones among the 'new men' have already perceived why those of refined sensibilities in previous generations have always understood the words of the psalmist conceived in another dry land, 'I am a sojourner here as all my fathers were.' The heroes of the people are now those who have learned to endure, with dignity and courage, the fate of being human beings in Australia.[20]*

Our Stories

One could add many other stories, individual, family and ethnic.[21] The issue, however, would seem more personal now. How do each of us tell our stories as Australians with such a past, in such a present and with what hopes for a common future? It will mean, of course, confessing our own Australian sins and protesting against the sins of other Australians—in that order![22] Evil in whatever form, if unnamed, continues to have power. Named, confessed, unmasked, it becomes a spur for some creative response, be it to forgiveness, to conversion, certainly to a larger compassion and responsibility. Most of all, it will mean owning the grace of our past. It has become a more or less set piece of recent Australian literature to satirise our past, especially the religious influences that went into it. Perhaps the majority of us have been typically inarticulate as Australians here. For many, priests, brothers and nuns were not life-denying ogres but sturdy human beings who put their lives, unpaid and unacknowledged, into caring for their people. I find myself with that question when I try to express my own story: is our current amazement at the greed and materialism of our present in no small way due to the legacy of love that has come from our past. The kinds of people that the 'Irish church' put in our paths when we were young, do not seem to be so numerous today. Who will the present generation have to satirise? But I don't want to sentimentalise, for after all, the shortcomings associated with the suspicions and defensiveness of the ghetto are obvious now.[23] Still, the question does gnaw away: Was all that generosity of family and dedication of religious people, merely to lead us into the promised land of *this*? Our past is at least partly a history of an altruism that suffered for our liberation from ignorance, prejudice and isolation. Is it not time for a far more generous way of imagining what really went on *in diebus illis*.[24]

Through it all, the forgotten or unspoken story of Australia occurs like a parable to upset the official version of what we are supposed to be. Like the gospel story it has an unsettling force. Once our history becomes the amnesia of a bland, grand success story, leaving out the memory of the despised and the forgotten, it is a defence against the past. The suffering is disowned; to recall it is unsettling; it is not worth the telling in our 'value-free' apprehension of today. But if we hear the story with a more compassionate imagination, it becomes a parable exploding our superficial myths of national success. In all the successive contexts of our search for a more hopeful future, it demands a hearing, as a past worth the telling. A pause occurs in our national conversation to allow the true story to be told. We have yet to absorb the depths of suffering and the heights of hope that are there to be expressed. The whole truth, in the end, is the only healing version of history.

It is in so many ways a story of suffering: Frayne flayed by the horrible 'cat', Facey nearly cut to death by the stockwhip, Daisy Corunna (Sally Morgan's grandmother) taken from her people, the generations of despised migrants...

Related to the Australian story is another story of suffering. It is the great parable of Jesus of Nazareth. A few decades ago theologians, suddenly made aware of the driven, hopeless irreligion of modern life, found in Nietzche's phrase the key to understanding the secularism of our times: 'God is dead'. But Australians knew all about that long before. Here faith was always underground. The 'God is dead' of Australian history is oddly linked with the dying of God in the passion of Christ. Christians, at least, can make the connection in their telling of the story of Australia in a way that inspires both hope and direction. Can Australia be a parable of humanity, heard with hope in the prisons, the killing fields, the Gulags of our time, as the story of the poor who got away to a place where human beings were finally treated as equals. As Les Murray has remarked, 'We began as the poor who were sent away, to England's South Sea Gulag, and our continent was largely settled by the poor who got away.'[25] To adapt a question that was asked about that master of parables, whose own life and death was the living parable for all ultimate human hope: Can any good come out of Australia?

Compared to 'the lush jungle of modern thought' such a past does seem like a desert. Yet in our efforts to retell our Australian story there are spirits to be summoned up challenging us to something more... 'if still from the deserts the prophets come'. (A. D. Hope)[26] And Francis Webb in 'Poet' can be taken to speak for each Australian when he writes:

> *I'm from the desert country—O, it's a holy land*
> *With a thousand warm humming stinging virtues.*[27]

If such an accommodation is acceptable, then the challenge is to retrieve the sense of the 'holy land' that nourished us, and to go on naming lovingly the thousand virtues that still hum somewhere in our consciousness, and sting our consciences. Who could say it better than a scholarly priest distinguished for his work both in Scripture, and in archaeology and for his championing of the Aboriginal cause:

> *But through all this, little Australia has struggled, has coped, has survived. This is the real story of our people. We have been taught another version: a succession of big names, a history of conquest of nature (and of man!) for monetary gain, the development of primary and secondary industries, growth of commerce and trade, involvement with international trading blocs. As successive election campaigns have shown, governments (and their coerced electorates) have been preoccupied with fiscal management, but the patient remains an economic hypochondriac, not only failing in his main intent, but sick in body and soul. Our country has been and continues to be portrayed as a business enterprise, Australia Incorporated but the Midas touch has turned warm human flesh and laughing eyes into chilling gold. Australia is far more than a commercial concern. It is a particular land and people, and it has a more human story. It is a tale about the majority of Australians, the little people, who can find their identity and unity around the indigenous core of trials and who, rather than the money changers, might yet be the foundation of a truly great people.*[28]

So, in the end, in this Australia, whose story do we listen to?

---

1. 'A Sense of Integrity' *Arena* 84, 1988, p. 98.
2. Robert Bellah, *The Broken Covenant*, Seabury, New York, 1976, p. 162.

3. For a concise and inspiring statement of the history of Australian Christianity, see Ian Breward, *Australia: The Most Godless Place under Heaven?*, Beacon Hill Books, Melbourne, 1988.

4. Patrick White, 'A Sense of Integrity', p. 99.

5. Manning Clark, 'Heroes', *Australia...*, p. 81.

6. Manning Clark, p. 81.

7. See Les Murray, 'Some religious Stuff I know about Australia', in *The Shape of Belief*, D. Harris, D. Hynd, D. Millikan (eds.), Lancer Books Anzea Publishers, 1982, p.17.

8. Penguin, Melbourne, 1982.

9. p. 314.

10. Jan Carter, 'Afterword', A. B. Facey, *A Fortunate Life*, Penguin, Melbourne, 1988, pp. 325–331.

11. p. 328f.

12. Reprinted from the Pan Books edition (London 1987) by permission of Collins Publishers.

13. pp. 463f.

14. p. 469.

15. p. 482.

16. From *My Place*, © Sally Morgan, Fremantle Arts Centre Press, 1987.

17. For example, pp. 102f, 227, 355; For Glad and Nan, pp. 242–244.

18. p. 213.

19. p. 350.

20. 'Heroes', p. 82.

21. Patrick O'Farrell, *The Irish in Australia*, Kensington: NSW, University Press, 1987.

22. See Denis Edwards, 'Sin and Salvation in the South Land of the Holy Spirit', *Discovering...*, pp. 89–102.

23. See Bruce Duncan's outstanding but as yet unpublished thesis, *From Ghetto to Crusade: A Study of the Social and Political Thought of Catholic Opinion-Makers in Sydney during the 1930s*, Dept. of Government, Sydney University, 1988; Edmund Campion, *Australian Catholics. The Contribution of Catholics to the Development of Australian Society*, Viking, Melbourne, 1987; and Paul Collins, *Mixed Blessings*, Penguin, Melbourne, 1986.

24. For an instructive way of reflecting on a variety of life-stories see Carmel Leavey OP and Margaret Hetherton, *Catholic Beliefs and Practices*, Collins Dove, Melbourne, 1988.

25. Murray, 1981, p. 17.

26. *Anthology...*, p. 228.

27.   *Anthology...*, p. 178. Reprinted from *Collected Poems*, © A. L. Meere, C. M. Snell, M. A. Webb-Wagg, 1973, by permission of Angus & Robertson Publishers/Collins.

28.   Eugene Stockton, 'Their Blackened Stump is Holy Seed', *Compass Theology Review* 22., Autumn-Winter, 1988, p. 24, by permission of the publisher.

Chapter 6:
The Land Held Holy

Australians lead a saucer-like existence, perched on the edge of their unruly continent and their lives are like exotic orchards which have no relationship to the wilderness stretching from rim to rim. They wear the profile for the vast unconscious to which some unknown genius gave the marvellously evocative name of the Never Never.
(John Olsen)[1]

With so many of us living in big cities, it is somewhat ironic that we Australians are growing in a feeling for our land, this unique continent. It is our place; the place where our lives are earthed and grounded. We are coming to reverence it as our own 'holy land'. As it supports and nourishes our lives, the environment enters into our very souls, as a symbol of common embodiment in this universe.

A New Dwelling in the Land

There are, doubtless, a number of reasons for this new sense of deeper belonging. We are learning a new appreciation of our land from the original Australians who in their 'Dreaming' see this part of the earth as a kind of great sacrament, a place of inexhaustible and original mystery. The growing ecological awareness makes us see how precious and how vulnerable it all is. Further, we catch from the thousands of tourists who come here a sense of the wonderland that happens to be our homeland. Most of all, so many of us have personally discovered something of our country's beauty and variety, in the rain forests and the Barrier Reef, Uluru and the great red country of the inland, the beaches and deserts, the open spaces. Across all ages and cultures it is something we have in common, to love, to explore, to enjoy.

Even if it took a hundred years before a recognisable gum tree appeared on a canvas, Australian painters have now learned to portray the land as a habitation of our spirit. Artists such as Heysen, Streeton, Nolan, Boyd, Pugh and Williams have made us see it as our own. They have captured its luminous spaces, its aridity, its desolation, its stark contrasts in colour and mood. The result is that Australians are deeply involved in redrawing the map of their country. We are trying to appreciate it as the terrain of more spiritual belonging. Calling a vast eastern stretch of this country 'New South Wales' is, I suppose, a hugely ironic tribute to the depths of nostalgia once felt for parent Britain. But some names can be changed. The great red rock at the centre of this country is once more Uluru. How a nineteenth-century English immigrant, Sir John Ayer, rose as a mining entrepreneur to be Governor of South Australia, and came to have Australia's most sacred site named after him, even though he never actually saw it, says a lot about the way Europeans possessed this land. Bruce Dawe, in his poem 'Credo', says it well:

> I am part of this bull-necked civilisation
> shoving its way across the country...
> —this is the Australian look we had before
> we were born, we grope
> over the face of this land with blind hands,
> guessing the features,
> a mouth, eyes, what could be a nose...we try
> to look content, not let down, not disappointed...[2]

Praying Here

The bread and wine of the Eucharist are offered to God as 'fruit of the earth and the work of human hands'. What is given back to us as the sacrament of the Lord's body and blood is what this land has produced—wheat and grapes harvested here, ripened under the Australian sun. Increasingly, our churches and liturgies try to include in the celebration of our faith the colours, the sounds, the fragrances, the spirit that comes from living here. For this land inspires its own psalms of praise as we enjoy God's creation and sense the presence of God's blessing in the colours that catch the eye, the bird songs we hear, the animals we are familiar with, the scents and fragrances of the bushland air, the blue sky of our days and the luminous stars of the inland sky, the great circling reality of our oceans, the silence and vastness of outback and desert. Our prayer is now much more inclined to rise up from where we are.

And I am fitted to that land as the soul is to the body,
I know its contractions, waste, and sprawling indolence;
They are in me and its triumphs are my own,
Hard-won in the thin and bitter years without pretence. [3]

Our souls are embodied in all this as symbols of the divine presence. It is almost as though the whole has become a vast 'sacred site' to be reverenced and shared in a new way.

A Violent Relationship

And yet there are serious, indeed, terrible conflicts and confusions in the way we are dwelling here. The empty beer can and cigarette pack wait for you in the places you most love. A willy-willy of food wrappers or a pile of plastic containers indicate other kinds of presence. The strange dye staining the water of the local creek is a sign of a deeper devastation, the outcome of a way of life that has not cared enough. We all know this dark other side: the polluted beaches, the hills and plains denuded of their trees, the erosion that scars the landscape, the 'die-back' in the forests and the salinity in the soil, the uncaring destruction of so much that was once so beautiful and is now irreplaceably gone. 'We came first as exiles, later as predators; love came late, if ever, and by the time we began to understand a little of the land, we had already set a pattern of destruction.' [4]

We could dismiss such statements as a romantic lament, the

soft-headed ineffectual or irresponsible protest of another 'greeny'. The pity is that Christians have so often seen no religious significance in what has been happening, as though we are so locked up in our souls that the land in which we are embodied is outside the domain of our conscience and the scope of our care.

Our earth and our land are given to us to nourish life, in body and in mind. Before it is farmland or a mine, before it is a timber to be logged and turned into woodchips, before it is property to be individually owned and commercially developed, it is our common homeland, a wonderland nourishing life in all its variety. Not to feel this, not to appreciate and to care this way leads inevitably to our land becoming a wasteland of exhausted soil, fouled water, stunted forests and hundreds, thousands of species of birds, fish, animals and plants threatened or made extinct for ever. How odd that we Australians need The World Heritage Organisation to remind us that what took millions of years in the making can pass seemingly unnoticed from the face of the earth, crushed in the path of the huge machine of modern technology.

A Neglected Conscience

As I say, it is strange that this has so little engaged the religious conscience. It would be judged monstrous if all the tender and passionate possibilities of exchange between human beings were reduced to rape. Yet that, in the area of our relationship to the land, is so often what has happened. Religious people should be alive to the gift of creation; Christians above all, intent on the love of their neighbour, know that it is no love to bequeath to future generations an exhausted and impoverished environment. Those whose faith is nourished by Christian sacraments can hardly be insensitive to the sacramentality of creation: there is no grace in a desecrated wasteland. Yet we have been slow learners here. Why are we not more obviously present in the ranks of those who are trying to educate our people and our government to a more tender, less violent and rapacious relationship to our land?

We have known a lot about how explorers, squatters, settlers, selectors, miners, loggers, farmers and graziers, city dwellers, developers and tourists have related to the land. It is now time to learn something else. Is there room for a more spiritual relationship? There has to be. An Australian poet wrote some years ago:

The country grows
Into the image of the people,
And the people grow
Into the likeness of the country
Till to the soul's geographer,
each becomes the symbol of the other. [5]

The interrelationship of land and people gives point to the situation we are now in. Through two centuries of European habitation, the country has grown into the image of the people. Such growth reveals a violent, uncaring, destructive ugliness. Two centuries have destroyed so much of what took two million years to produce.

If we, the people 'grow into the likeness of the country', there is, one must fear, much to ponder: the good possibilities are that we become a people of space, where silences can flourish, in which we can relate to our land in reverence and tenderness as we treasure all the varied wonder of its life. The sadder possibilities are there too, in what has already taken place. We can look at what we have destroyed. We can see the polluted beaches and the many paths of our careless exploitation. Is it an expression of an inner wasteland that has brought all this about? Is an exhausted and threatened land a symbol of what we have become?

Humility

The issue is, to my mind, a religious one. To learn humility. The Latin word derives from *humus*, the soil, the earth. An essential part of our humanity is to accept the earth from which we come and to care for it as our living environment. We are not meant to be pure spirits haunting the face of an exhausted land, but persons embodied in an earth, 'earthed' in that sense, accepting its limitations and rejoicing in its web of delicate life. In this century, we have come to appreciate how vulnerable and beautiful is this planet we share. In our way, we Australians have to reclaim our land, to belong to it, to dwell in it, to receive from it and give back to it in exchanges of care and tenderness.

In a word, to possess it more spiritually in a reverence we can well learn from the original inhabitants. As Judith Wright puts it:

> The land we occupied less than two hundred years ago has been decisively and immensely altered during that time. Australians of European or Asian descent may never attain the kind of intimate relationship with it that so many millennia have given to its Aboriginal inhabitants. But a growth of attachment on grounds not wholly economic is perceptible already, and may finally bring the two viewpoints a little closer if real action is taken to heal the wounds we have dealt both to the land and to its original owners.[6]

On one of the great freeways linking two of our cities there is a happily phrased sign on the median strip, 'Reserved for Native Regeneration'. For all I know, the local shire did not have the resources to keep it neatly mown. Whatever the case, the sign expresses quite accurately, if unwittingly, a programme for the whole of Australia!

A great Australian novelist wrote these words in one of his books:

> Everyman has a genius, though it is not always discoverable. Least of all when choked by the trivialities of daily existence. But in this disturbing country ..it is possible more easily to discard the inessential and to attempt the infinite.[7]

That, really, does appear to be the issue. The challenge upon us is to appreciate our land as a great sacrament of providence uniting us as one community in this time, this place; to hold this land in sacred trust as a homeland for future generations of all the kinds of life that thrive here. If we come to possess a deeper reverence for this land, it will be a blessing to say 'The country grows/ Into the image of the people/ And the people grow /Into the likeness of the country'. If conscience fails, it will be a curse.

All this invites us to be more deeply attentive to the immemorial words of another poet who preached that we had something to learn from the lilies of the field and the birds of the air.

---

1. John Olsen, *The Land beyond Time: Paintings and Drawings by John Olsen*, The Art Gallery of Western Australia, 1984, p. 8.
2. Bruce Dawe, 'Credo', quoted in Peter Kirkwood, 'Two Australian Poets as

Theologians: Les Murray and Bruce Dawe', *Compass Theology Review* 19, Autumn 1985, p. 32.

3.   James McAuley, 'Envoi'. Reprinted from *Collected Poems 1930–70*, © Norma McAuley, 1971, by permission of Angus and Robertson Publishers/Collins.

4.   Judith Wright, 'Landscape and Dreaming', *Australia...*, p. 52.

5.   Max Dunn, *Portrait of a Country*, Melbourne, 1962, p. 14.

6.   Judith Wright, 'Landscape and Dreaming', *Australia...*, p. 55.

7.   Patrick White, *Voss*, London, Jonathan Cape, 1957, p. 38, reprinted by permission of the publisher.

Chapter 7: Their Place

Our country seems to have come to a remarkable turning point in recent years. Indeed, conversion is not too strong a word. It has to do with the place of Aboriginal Australians in our national consciousness. It is not just a matter of recognising their political, economic or cultural rights. It is more positive—a conscious, more open, responsive living with, and learning from, this land's original people. It is the beginnings of something like a spiritual partnership, more like a shared pilgrimage into the future of this continent.

Too little, too late? Many mistakes have been made, many sins committed; and there is much sorrow and regret. But even a little is something compared with the neglect and violent exclusion of the past. Even though it has been a slow learning that has brought us to this point, it is never too late to learn a larger humanity and deeper spiritual kinship. For this continent contains us all. It brings us together. It makes us face one another. We have nowhere else to go.

To be at this point has taken time, and time has taken its toll. At the beginning there was the uncomprehending curiosity of the first white settlers and convicts two hundred years ago as they met a strange new race. It was an irony that some of these isolated and degraded Europeans, themselves casualties of an inhuman system, should doubt the humanity of the Aboriginal people. After all, the original inhabitants of this land had, up to that point, neither suffered nor inflicted the degradations that these late arrivals took for granted as part of civilisation. What was clear was the difference between these two groups of human beings. History was about to witness a horrifying clash of cultures. An age-old culture, far more spiritual than what was now threatening it, was about to enter into a tragic time of vulnerability. In essence, it was the vulnerability of a larger humanity: 'The genius of their society lay in other directions and it was this otherness, fundamentally, that led to their undoing.'[1]

Initial curiosity soon yielded to hostility. With the expansion of the settlement, competition for the land began. With the establishment of colonial power, what followed was systematic neglect and exclusion. A useful amnesia developed: some crimes were too terrible to admit. Slowly, with the development of social conscience, helped in various ways by the missions, the Aborigines became a 'problem'. And so began the varied and often drastic efforts to solve this 'Aboriginal problem'. Essentially, it had been created by the original illegal expropriation of Aboriginal land and its owners' consequent defenceless exposure to alien forces. But now, the creators of the problem saw themselves as the makers of the solution. Today, despite such a history, something different is taking place.

This current phase began with the granting of the rights of citizenship only twenty years ago. It developed with the often grudging recognition of land rights. It is flowering into an era of partnership based on a positive appreciation of the Aboriginal presence, and even deference to Aboriginal leadership.

The dawning of this appreciation of Aboriginal history as essential to the future of bicentennial Australia has to contend with the sad narrative of invasion, banishment, exclusion, domination and prejudice. Yet there are glimmerings of reconciliation based on a firmer justice.

So, a lot has changed. Many Australians of Aboriginal extraction can rejoice in finding 'their place'—not to be kept there, but as the point of proud and hopeful belonging. This is wonderfully expressed in Sally Morgan's *My Place*, which I referred to in Chapter 5. It recounts how this young Perth woman searches out her Aboriginal roots. Her exploration reveals the extraordinary patience, the sufferings, the humour, the faith and the remarkable sense of community characteristic of her people.

In such a discovery the rest of us find something more wonderful about 'our place' as well. When Aboriginal Australia finds its place, it is experienced as something of a homecoming for the rest of us Australians with our varied English, Irish, European and Asian origins. For it is a spiritual event. It is a healing that comes from justice. It is a renewed attunement to the wonders of this land we share. Most deeply, it is the occurrence of a new sense of community in the common task of building a future in a world threatening to all. If, in the judgment of a revered authority, 'the aboriginal religion was probably the least material-minded and the most life-minded of any of which we have knowledge',[2] any religion, struggling in the obsessive materialism of our day, has to sense that there is a lot to be learned in a larger ecology of Australian awareness. What the Aboriginal contribution to the larger ecology of awareness might be is tellingly expressed by Eugene Stockton:

In the harshest continent on earth, they learnt to survive by entering into partnership with the land which became a whole way of life, a spirituality. Spiritual development was preferred to the technological in satisfying the basic needs and higher aspirations of a society, moulded as it was like no other and over a greater stretch of time in the matrix of a mothering land.[3]

I use the word 'ecology' advisedly in referring to our national awareness. The physical problems of the despoiled environment objectify the limitations of the stunted inner landscape. Max Dunn's poem asserts that 'The country grows/ Into the image of the people,/ And the people grow/ Into the likeness of the country'.[4] The inner and outer ecologies interrelate as to the 'soul's geographer' each becomes the symbol of the other. A 'bull-necked civilisation' (Dawe) has its consequences. What there is to be learned is suggested by the words of the Aboriginal artist, Wandjuk Marika:

This land is not empty, the land is full of knowledge, full of story, full of goodness, full of energy, full of power. The earth is our mother, the land is not empty. There is the story I am telling you—special, sacred, important.[5]

I hope Aboriginal Australians will be patient with the rest of us. The well-meaning will tend to romanticise a bit and perhaps lose sight of the challenges that still remain. Still, it is difficult to deny that a decisive turning point in our history has been reached. Evidently some new grace is stirring.

The continuing, almost miraculous Aboriginal presence in Australia takes us to a special limit in our experience of humanity and its history. Next to our two hundred years of occupancy of this continent, their forty thousand years is all but overwhelming. F.T. Macartney's 'Didjeridoo' captures a Euro-pean sense of bewilderment at this uncanny expanse of history:

> *Didjeridoo-didjeridoo!*
> *A nursery rhyme and a history too.*
> *Black faces lean over a flickering fire;*
> *A nasal chant rises, drops low, rises higher,*
> *Then wearily fades to an echo of wind*
> *Over withering grasses that footsteps have thinned*
> *Through nomadic ages, space without scope,*
> *Unscarred by regret, unharassed by hope;*
> *For primitive ages are distanced into*
> *A groan to the bone by the didjeridoo.*

Aboriginal Australians stand in a largely unknown, mysterious stretch of history preceding even the larger background of ethnic and cultural histories of most Australians by thirty-five millennia.

> *Didjeridoo-didjeridoo!*
> *Even the pastorals, lyric with dew,*
> *Piped in Arcadian meadows so green*
> *And so golden and glad and so mythically clean,*
> *Are not so remote as this shudder of sound,*
> *Which broods like a beast nuzzling close to the ground*
> *For the track of its mate or an answering wail.*
> *The piper sits playing and knows all things fail.*
> *The days are so many, the years are so few,*
> *Says the thud, as of mud, in the didjeridoo.*[6]

The extent of Aboriginal history leads us all into a wonderment, a 'dreaming' if we can borrow their word, about human time and providence that has worked in all peoples, to bring us together in this critical moment in our country's history. The dimensions of such a past make way for a new kind of future in which we might be more capable of greeting the humanness in one another as a gift and to learn a larger, less violent humanity.

Miriam Rose Ungunmerr testifies to the deep spiritual resources that are part of the Aboriginal tradition.[7] She appreciates that many Australians have learned from Aboriginals a 'special respect for Nature. The identity we have with the land is sacred and unique...Aboriginal people have a very strong sense of community. All persons matter. All of us belong...we are a people who celebrate together.' Yet she singles out one special gift, *dadirri*—a kind of contemplation, 'an inner deep listening, and quiet, still awareness'. It is the source of continuing spiritual renewal, a relatedness to the source of life. She quotes Pope John Paul II's words in this context, 'You lived your lives in spiritual closeness to the land... Through this closeness to the land, you touched the sacredness of man's relationship to God, for the land was the proof of a power of life greater than yourselves...' She explains how her people are not threatened by this silence, and how their fundamental religiousness, was arguably 'the least material-minded, and the most life-minded' of any we know.

The secret of this is the waiting, listening quality, content to stay close to the mystery of life and its source—to be 'ab-Original' in the most literal sense. Her hope is that the rest of Australians will learn not so much to 'wait for' the Aboriginal people but to 'wait with them' in the interests of a deeper attunement to the spiritual. Miriam Rose Ungunmerr has the hope that this kind of listening 'will blossom and grow, not just within ourselves, but in our whole nation'.[8]

Admittedly, this continuing and growing Aboriginal presence in Australian society is unsettling too. For it embodies forever in our national conscience a challenge to the brutal greed that all but destroyed them. It is the dangerous memory of what was once 'otherwise'. Aboriginal Australians stand at the jagged edge of many of the questions we are now asking: How do they invite us beyond materialism to a deeper spiritual culture? How does such a presence stretch the exploitative imagination to form an economy at home in the ecology of this land? How does their experience of 'sacred sites' awaken us to a range of values rather different from the concerns of the mining corporation and the real estate developer? The 'breadth' of European experience is challenged by the 'length and depth' of another way of being in the world. In Aboriginal experience and history, the Australia of this late (post?) Christian era is offered another 'Old Testament' of covenant and holiness in which to imagine a new hope.

A timely collection of Aboriginal verse has appeared this year, called, appropriately, *Inside Black Australia*.[9] It is edited by the well-known Aboriginal writer, Kevin Gilbert. Poetry is uniquely the language of the heart, and of the heart's deepest experiences of sorrow, joy and belonging. The dozens of poems collected here reveal many facets of Aboriginal contemporary experience. What one notices again and again is the deep criticism of the inhumanity of the dominant culture. To read such poems is an examination of conscience:

> *When vile men jeer because my skin is brown,*
> *This I live down.*
> *But when a taunted child comes home in tears,*
> *Fierce anger sears.*
>
> *The Christianity you hold so high*
> *Is but a lie.*[10]

These few verses from Kath Walker's (Oodgeroo Noonuccal) 'Colour Bar' stab at the heart of racism in Australia and the suffering it has caused. On the other side of such sensitivity is the Aboriginal's criticism of Australian culture. It exposes the compulsions and myths of ourselves as 'the unhappy race'. The Myall speaker ends with the words:

> *Leave us alone. We don't want your collars and ties,*
> *We don't need your routines and compulsions.*
> *We want the old freedom and joy that all things have but you,*
> *Poor white man of the unhappy race.*[11]

Another Aboriginal poet, Jim Everett ponders 'the white man problem'—rather a reversal of the usual situation. He laments that 'few whites want' to learn the more human ways of the Aborigines. The poem deplores the inhumanity and hypocrisy of white civilisation with its reliance on technological power, and ends with the words:

> *The answer must be that whites with power*
> *Exploit the poor and down of their own kin.*
> *That dog eat dog is white history known,*
> *That the white man's problem is not just his skin.*[12]

As I say, something important is happening to Australian consciousness. It has to expand to a different perception of life, to accept a criticism of so much of our acquisitive culture, to confess the sins of bicentennial history...to allow for something new. Perhaps it will come as the answer to the Aboriginal prayer:

Father,
you gave us the Dreaming.
You have always spoken to us
through our belief.
You then made your love clear to us
in the message of Jesus.
We thank you for your care.
You own us, you are our hope!
Make us strong as we face the problem of change.
We ask you to help the people of Australia to listen to us and respect
our belief.

We can only know you and ourselves
in our culture.
Make the knowledge of you grow
strong in all people so that you can find
a home in us
and we can make a home
for everyone in our land.[13]

---

1.   W. Stanner, *After the Dreaming*, The 1968 Boyer Lectures, Sydney, 1969, p. 42.

2.   Stanner, p. 119.

3.   Stockton, p. 21.

4.   *Portrait of a Country*, Melbourne, 1962, p. 14.

5.   *Long Water: Aboriginal Art and Literature*, Bathurst, 1978, p. 9.

6.   *Anthology...*, p. 181. Reprinted from *Selected Poems*, © F. T. Macartney by permission of Angus & Robertson Publishers/Collins.

7.   'Dadirri', *Compass Theology Review* 22, Autumn 1988, pp. 9–11. See also the articles in the same issue by D. Gondarra and Patrick Dodson.

8.   Miriam Rose Ungunmerr, p. 11.

9.   Kevin Gilbert (ed.), *An Anthology of Aboriginal Poetry*, Penguin, Melbourne, 1988.

10.   Kath Walker, 'Colour Bar', in Gilbert, p. 96.

11.   'The Unhappy Race', in Gilbert, p. 96.

12.   Jim Everett, 'The White Man Problem', in Gilbert, p. 106.

13.   *Anthology...*, pp. 191–192.   This prayer, written by members of the Aboriginal Catholic community in Alice Springs, was used on the occasion of the recent papal visit, at Alice Springs 1 November 1986.

Chapter 8:
Australian Mysticism

Uluru is the articulate heart of Australia. It speaks to all of us. Its sure and solid foundation makes it a rock of refuge, a sacred place of worship, of struggle between good and evil and a resort for the hot, the weary and the thirsty. Guides tell the visitor that aboriginal groups could see the Rock from far away and, especially in times of drought, journey towards its shade, its beautiful sheltering clefts, drink from the pools. But they then moved on; others might want to come to be refreshed in this place. There is life around the Rock. The desert is arid but not barren. Bird-life, animals, desert trees and shrubs and, after rain, grasses and flowers...

Uluru invites Australians to centre themselves, to reflect, to be aware of a presence in our land which transcends ourselves, which is godly. In the desert, the longings of the Australian heart can surface, be expressed, and find some hope and reassurance. As aborigines did in the past, back we go to our own places, back to the coast and the hinterland. Can we ponder all these things in our hearts? We must not be amongst those who have the experience but miss the meaning. (Peter Malone)[1]

Here we reflect on the explicitly mystical, the religious character of Australian experience. In the great theatre of our world's variety of experience, the story of radical spirituality is told in many languages and accents.[2] Traditional European theology has usually told the story of our human experience of God's grace in terms of 'salvation'. The Christian people of Central and South America today express it in terms of 'liberation' from a past that has structured the evils of the present. The emphasis of Asia is on 'revelation'—God as the light of life. In North America, with the USA as 'the Land of the Free', the accent is on freedom and the meaning of God as the ground and goal of human rights. Perhaps the most consistent accent of Africa, with its dance and art and its exuberant corporate sense, is Incarnation, the fullness of life. We might, then, wonder what is the pattern of Australian religious experience in the varied context of the world of grace. What is our own sense of God? Is there an Australian brand of mysticism?

Once more we are teased by one of those intense words more at home in the Rhineland of the Middle Ages or in the monasteries of sixteenth-century Spain. It is transposed oddly into the context of Down Under. The 'Kingdom of Nothingness' (Manning Clark) may have its positive side: the 'No-Thing' that evades all expression and embodiment, and yet remains the mystery relativising everything and inviting us to something more.

The Data

Murray's 'wholespeak' lives from a deep awareness of the whole experienced as No-thing—nothing that can be summed up, manipulated, reduced to something else—the mystery which abides. Aboriginal Dreaming lives from the people's experience of the Origin and its all-embracing continuing influence through the sacramentality of the land. 'Ab-origin-ality' has a deeper sense if you take it this way, in a religious, rather than in the usual anthropological, sense. Such a sense of mysterious origin is registered in Aboriginal consciousness as the habit of *dadirri*, or meditation, as I have already referred to in Miriam Rose Ungunmerr's reflections.[3] In a different language, it is the elusive unfading flower of 'the truth' from which all the variety of world emerges, as it is expressed in Judith Wright's poem 'The Forest', just as it is the cosmic 'rhythm which dances and is not mine' in her 'Five Senses'.[4] It is the all-inclusive mystery founding the compassion of Bruce Dawe's 'Prayer for those in Coma'.[5] It is 'the meaning, not ours/

but found...' in Jim McAuley's 'Credo'.[6] Anyone reading Murray's *Anthology of Australian Religious Poetry* can find rich data for spiritual and theological reflection.[7]

Then, to give a couple of examples from Australian novels,[8] we see this mystical dimension in Patrick White's *Tree of Man*: Stan's 'gob of spittle' ironically contrasts with the urgent verbosity of the young evangelist:

> *A great tenderness of understanding rose in his chest. Even the most obscure, the most sickening incidents of his life were clear. In that light, 'How long will they leave me like this,' he wondered, in peace and understanding?*

Very evocatively, it is suggested by the quiet Tom Spring in Randolph Stow's *Tourmaline*, as he tries to find words for what cannot be expressed:

> *...and he did try. But so stumblingly, so clumsily, that it was difficult to attend. He unveiled his God to mean his God had names like the nameless, the sum of all, the ground of being. He spoke of the unity of opposites and the overwhelming power of inaction. He talked of becoming a stream, to carve out canyons without ceasing to yield, of being a tree to grow without thinking; of being a rock to be shaped by winds and tides. He said I must become empty in order to be filled, must unlearn everything, must accept the role of fool. And with curious fumbling passion he told me of a gate leading into darkness, which was both a valley and a woman, the source and the sap of life, the temple of revelation. At moments, I thought I glimpsed through the inept words, something of his vision of fullness and peace, the power and the darkness. Then, it was obscured again, hidden behind his battles with the language, and I understood nothing, nothing at all...*

Solitude

In such varied testimony, a deep mystical current struggles for expression in the literary creativity of some of our writers. It is characterised by an earthy, tentative quality rather than by a dramatic inrush of revelation. This, no doubt, has something to do with the larger cultural pattern of Australian experience. The religious dimension appears as a precious secret rather than as the open confession of more explicitly religious cultures. Henry S. Albinsky, gives a reason for our more prosaic, less 'divinely elected' consciousness when he writes:

> *While American culture evolved a myth of equality, of the process of opportunity—from rags to riches, from log cabin to White House—equality's texture in Australia became one simply of being...it declared, in effect, live and let live and allow a fair go: far more prosaic impulses than life, liberty and the pursuit of happiness.*[9]

Such a fundamental contrast between Australia and the United States, helps explain a different kind of religiousness. Americans tend naturally to locate religion in terms of great public national enterprise, sanctioning the pursuit of life, liberty and happiness. Australians in their 'live and let live' attitude tend to see it as a private, more interior, less expressible matter. For North Americans, God is the guarantor of the public order and the American dream of freedom for all under God. For Australians, God is the one who guarantees individuality and a right to live somewhat outside the system, even in opposition to it.

But such intense individualism is at a price. It has to face its own kind of existential panic. Patrick White muses:

> *A great number of Australians seem to be running to or from somewhere—city to surf in my native city—capital to capital—sometimes in the name of charity or to advertise a product...this passion for perpetual motion—is it perhaps a fear that we may have to sit down and face reality if we don't keep going?*[10]

Then, as I mentioned in Chapter 2, the nakedness and confusion of the Australian soul are expressed by the woman traveller in Murray Bail's *Homesickness* as she confesses, 'We come from a country...of nothing really, or at least of nothing substantial yet...'[11]

In such a context, the good heart seemingly has no where to go. It is a rootlessness looking for some deeper belonging. Indeed, to return to Patrick White, his words, on his return to Australia to write the *Tree of Man*, further express the 'unbearable lightness of being' Australian:

> *In all directions stretched the Great Australian Emptiness in which the mind is the least of possessions. It was the exaltation of the average that made me panic most, and in this frame of mind, in*

spite of myself, I began to conceive another novel. Because the void I had to fill was so immense, I wanted to try to suggest in this book every possible aspect of life, through the lives of an ordinary man and woman. But at the same time, I wanted to discover the extraordinary behind the ordinary, the mystery and the poetry which alone could make bearable the lives of such people, and incidentally, my own life since its return.[12]

When Australian culture has so resolutely opted for the ordinary, it seems that the 'extraordinary', 'the mystery and the poetry', require vigorous and discerning effort if they are to be expressed and experienced.

Search for the Centre

Still, such a sense of nakedness and isolation provokes its own creativity. If as a people we lack 'the continuity and congruency of land, population, history, tradition, and language that knit together a people's soul'[13], that very lack makes us search for the 'no-thing' that is the one thing necessary. A search for that ever-elusive centre becomes the great Australian dream. The ill-fated explorers of our early European history found only the desert of the interior. They could not have realised that, at a later stage of Australian consciousness, this 'dead heart' would become a rich spiritual symbol of space and freedom. This is realised above all in Uluru. It has become a central symbol for black and white Australians alike. It stands as a focus of a special kind of interior exploration. In a country whose dominant life-style has been formed by those who have clung to the peripheries of the continent, the mysterious centre has drawn many to a sense of a radical spiritual pilgrimage:

Recurrent metaphors of heart, soul and centre reflect the geographical peculiarity of a country that is most knowable at its peripheries. Much Australian writing reveals a deep yearning for unity, perhaps as a recompense for the breaking of bonds in the original severance from the old home, and the disruptive, violent arrival in the new. Centre-seeking is a leitmotif in Australian culture whether it is the impulse to align the experience of the new society with the central traditions and values of the old world, or a search for a new centre in the new land. The singleness of the island-continent makes a longing for the centre look feasible. Yet it is an aspiration of the most difficult metaphysical kind. It is a vision of a transcendent harmony between nature and nurture, between the 'untouched' land and what 'civilisation brings to it, between present selves and an enormous pluralistic cultural past. It is a grandiose dream on the scale of the land itself, an embryonic dream of imperium in which all are forerunners.[14]

It is indeed a pilgrimage 'of a most difficult metaphysical kind'. That is precisely the challenge of spirituality and the ethical and poetical imagination it supports. The above-quoted author barely alludes to the radically spiritual nature of our 'centre-seeking'. One hopes, at this critical stage, that dreams of *imperium*, however embryonic, are not the inspiring motive. The land is not just there as a resource to be conquered and developed. For there is the deeper matter of belonging to it in a spiritual way. Peter Malone catches the spirit of this new symbolic appreciation of the land as it is occurring in the often inarticulate Australian heart:

Australia is blessed with a symbolic heart, the great red monolith in the centre, Uluru. It stands in a motionless, timeless landscape, imaging eternity. Perhaps thrust across the plains by a genesis cataclysm, it stands with majestic strength, a centring place for all to come to. Aborigines traditionally journeyed to this rock refuge and sanctuary in times past. Now it belongs to them again. But now, too, pilgrims, be they reverent travellers or rushing tourists, from all over Australia are able to travel to the Rock.[15]

Searching for centre, knowing it is there, finding it, journeying back to the periphery, are all aspects of any pilgrimage through both the local and the spiritual landscape. An awareness of the real centre makes one more conscious of being on the margins. It cannot but make you more sensitive to those who dwell with you on the fringe. We begin to feel how we are displaced, 'off-centre', by a life-style more organised around self-centredness than the real centre of things, more concerned to be defensively self-enclosed than self-transcending into the real proportions of soul and land. Hence the spiritual quest, in its integrity, is both a faith and a compassion, a coming home and an endless setting out, an awareness of the eternal and a renewed return to the everyday. It is not surprising, then, to find that an astute commentator makes exactly this point about Australian consciousness in the context of recent Australian literature:

> *Yet here is the irony. If Australianness is elusive as a centre, an essence, a destiny, it is everywhere to be found as a refracting perspective, a melange, a quirk. The baffling circumstances that defeat the search for a centre may well prove to be the thing itself, and to think appreciatively in those terms may well be the first step away from mythology to the maturity that can rescue Australians from comic afflatus as well as tragic delusion.*[16]

Beyond the Periphery

The warning is there. The search is 'of a most difficult metaphysical kind'. It is a matter of getting beyond the fixation of the image to the indefinable reality. It is the challenge of nurturing an immediate sense of God in all the mediations of the land's symbols, but of resisting being trapped in them, so as to live in the 'in-between'. Les Murray has offered a timely warning here in his 'The Gravy in Images'[17] as does the great philosopher of history, Eric Voegelin.[18] What the theological tradition has called the 'via negativa', the way of negation serving a larger apprehension, must eventually come into play. If we are to avoid an idolatrous fixation in our own symbols, especially national symbols, there must be a time for iconoclasm. One aspect of the atmosphere of true imagination must be the 'cloud of unknowing'.

The special necessity of both this breaking of images and the 'unknowing' emerges today because of the texture of cultural communication. So much of our world is electronically 'mediated'—literally, through the media. As Donald Horne has pointed out, the modern media tend to take over the role of religion.[19] Such 'media-tions' throw up a regular 'map' of reality, telling us what things are like, what is worth talking about, what is normal, what is, and is not, possible. The media might not have the power to tell us what to think, but they have been 'stunningly successful in telling people what to think about'. The 'mediations' of the mass media work powerfully to make meditation, true thinking, impossible. Prefabricated images swamp the capacities of a larger imagination.

Such a state of affairs is all too easily verifiable. The only way in which human consciousness can keep its poise and direction today is through the spiritual power of true imagination. Such imagination, both ethical and poetical, lights the way from 'comic afflatus' to ironic humour, from tragic delusion into a sense of solidarity with the suffering other. By imagining the world otherwise, we can begin the radical questioning of alienated individualism and the images that pander to it. And in that world seen otherwise, mind and heart expand to a passion which 'bears all things, believes all things, hopes all things, endures all things' (I Cor. 13:7).

The Self's Self

In keeping with the spiritual rather than formally theological orientation of our reflections, I have been accenting the quality and governing symbols of our mystical experience. In a way, I have been stressing merely the need to reclaim in a conscious, critical manner the full experience of our historical and cultural selfhood, the full dimensions of our Australian awareness. Only in such a context can the specifically theological reality of God be meaningfully expressed. Ultimate objectivity, to adapt an axiom of Bernard Lonergan, is the fruit of authentic subjectivity. The more we are in touch with our deepest questions, feelings, moral aspirations and future hopes, the more the question of God makes sense. Religious education and communication must absorb this fundamental principle: God can be meaningfully affirmed only as the ground and goal of our most authentic selves in all their individual, social and global dimensions. The neglect of this principle has caused 'God in Australia' to be so often presented as a foreign and oppressive reality.By implication, God is the inevitable question for Australians if they dare to touch any of the limits I referred to in Chapter 2. Such limits provoke an anticipation of ultimate meaning and value. They make us imagine the world otherwise. Such an imagination unsettles the superficial and the routine. It airs the forgotten and disowned areas of our souls.

When something genuinely mystical stirs within us—and who is to say it does not, when we look at the wealth of Australian poetry, literature, painting, music, religious and social commitment—we find witnesses to a great humanising force at work. It is already enabling many to break out of the dead ends of all the disillusionment modern Australia is experiencing. Resistance has already begun against the suffocating banality that would replace the joy of life with consumer-designed fun; against the corrupting power of organised crime extending into all our institutions; against the concentration of power in the hands of the immensely rich; against the many-sided despair in those who still lovingly remember, or hopefully dream of, another Australia. Lonergan's lapidary expression once more says it all:

> As the question of God is implicit in all our questioning, so being in love with God is the basic fulfilment of our conscious intentionality. That fulfilment brings a deep-set joy that can remain despite humiliation, failure, privation, pain, betrayal, desertion. That fulfilment brings a radical peace, the peace the world cannot give. That fulfilment bears fruit in a love of one's neighbour that strives mightily to bring about the kingdom of God on earth. On the other hand, the absence of that fulfilment opens the way to the trivialisation of human life in the pursuit of fun, to the harshness of human life arising from the ruthless exercise of power, to despair about human welfare springing from the conviction that the universe is absurd.[20]

The God of our Silence

Then there is the mystery of God. Despite the towering integrity of his life, old Bert Facey expressed a violent rejection of God, or at least the notion of God our culture fed him. This is the case with a lot of Australians: a good instinct... breaking the graven images: God cannot be what we easily talk about. Even Thomas Aquinas said we can only know what God is not! Before him, the Bible reminds us, 'God dwells in inaccessible light' (I Tim. 6:16) and that 'no one has ever seen God' (Jn. 1:18)! Mystics speak of the 'cloud of unknowing'; John of the Cross kept repeating his *Nada*, '...nothing, nothing, nothing, and even on the mountain, nothing'. The Australian poems and novels already referred to often eloquently express the essentially indefinable character of the ultimate. Our inarticulateness is here very appropriate. Besides we have our own Australian antipathies to a religion that has sanctioned the monstrosities of Norfolk Island and provoked the bitterness of sectarianism.

But 'God'? The 'no-thing'... But to say nothing can appear to be agnostic or atheist. Such a discretion permits the silences we cherish to be filled up with the persistent inanity of the idols of consumerism. And they demand their own kind of human sacrifice as their devotees dance in an endless frenzy to the ad-man's jingle. So, the real God? It is true we must not say too much. Christians have to keep reminding themselves that God is known only by participating in the divine love-life in some way: 'Beloved, let us love one another for love is of God, and he who loves is born of God and knows God' (I Jn. 4:7). This passage precludes the self-absorbed religion that imagines we love God because we love no one. More positively, it witnesses to the God to be known only as the ground, the space, the horizon of our ultimate solidarity, the mystery intimated in all compassion.

The God of our Belonging

Given the Christian resources of our country, it is time to emphasise that the experience of God is pre-eminently a social experience.[21] God is the ultimate how and why and goal of our belonging together. The divine is the indefinable mystery in which we all belong, connecting us with one another in mutual responsibility. The Holy Spirit is the shared breath of our common humanity. Christ is the divine expression of compassionate humanness. The Father is the mystery in which we all come home. In all the classic expressions of Christian faith, the social and cosmic dimensions await a larger imagination. Isolated individualism is, in Christian terms, the practical expression of atheism.

This does not, of course, mean that we need to downplay those individual intimations of the divine that can come to us in the silence of a bushland morning, in our first vision of the Rock, in the wonder we feel under the stars of the Southern night, in the roll of the great surf, in the inspiration of our great poets, painters, musicians. The ethical, as I said before, needs the full play of the imagination! For each such experience invites to a sense of the wonder of a universe which is immediately given to us as shared, not owned by any individual, involving us all. Wholeness invades such private moments with a summons to belong to the all. It is the primordial sense of the common good in which all of us have a place.

If it is to be a common good from which no one is excluded it cannot be merely a project to be engineered by the knowing and powerful. Nor is it something designed by our economic or political masters; not something imposed by the censorious wowser who has forgotten the proportions of human wholeness. We are not raw material to be shaped by someone else's ambitions. It is about a common good for us, for us the people, and all of us together. Its symbol may well be, at Les Murray's suggestion, 'the common dish':

> ...*that vessel of common human sufferings, joys, disappointments, tragedies and bare sufficiencies from which most people have to eat in this world, and from which some choose to eat in order to keep faith with them. This dish is the opposite to the medieval Grail, which was a vessel attained only by a spiritual elite. To refuse the common ration, or to fail at least to recognise and respect it, earns one the contempt and rejection of battlers and all who have lived under the laws of necessity. It is a harsher vessel than the Christian chalice, and not identical with it, except perhaps for the saints, but I believe it lies close to the heart of Australian consciousness, and can never be safely ignored. It is the fountainhead of much of the conformity so often deplored in our society, and much of the art of living in Australia consists in judging, continually and possibly gracefully, just what distance we may wander from the common table and how often to come back.*[22]

Perhaps that is what is hidden in our myths of 'mateship', our pride in the attitude of 'live and let live', our sympathy for the underdog, the way the symbols of Gallipoli and Eureka are valued in our history. The truly human happens when we live through the solidarity of suffering. It inspires no theory about our common humanity, but more a conversation around a common dish, in which those who suffer have the best stories to tell. Something elementally human happens between human beings when they enter into one another's sufferings. That is when 'something' is revealed which graciously holds us together, connecting us responsibly with one another in truly human commonwealth.

The God of our Future

To avoid one more ideology of privilege, one more religious bigotry, one more technological manipulation, demands participation in a conversation about ultimate hopes: what we are against implies some sense of what, however inarticulately, we might be for. The mark of such a conversation is its refusal to regard the suffering as irrelevant. It resolutely lets everyone have their say and belong. In principle it is unconditional. Just as no one, no group, no race can be sacrificed to the interests of another, none can be excluded from the human conversation. To exclude anyone is to mutilate the human reality of what Australia is.

Hence consensus about our future is the ideal. It is a vigorous, informed conspiracy to subvert what is unjust and oppressive in our past and in our present. The only foundation for this is in the seemingly defenceless exchanges of a conversation based on telling the truth as we see it, above all the truth of real suffering, and beginning to imagine our world otherwise. Its aim is not to have power over others, Rather, it is a matter of empowering everyone to be part of a joint enterprise in the forming of a common future.

Those most voiceless are left out of the usual success story, yet, though most silent in determining the way things have gone, they occupy the privileged place. Why? Because they are least affected by the blandishments of the reigning ideologies of partisan politics, just as they are least bolstered by the rewards of the economic establishment, and most nakedly exposed in the essence of their humanity to the essential crisis affecting everyone: suffering, death, limitation, the question of our real worth.

What, then, is the significance of this sense of solidarity, this space of communication open to everyone but privileging the voices of those most forgotten and powerless? Does not such an open, inclusive conversation implicitly anticipate 'the structure of the real', the ultimate reality of our belonging together? To envisage such an ultimate consensus looks to the grace of 'no-thing', something that is not yet, an image of social belonging inviting us into a new kind of future.

Here, it seems to me, the Judaeo-Christian tradition has a valuable opportunity. It has the resources to articulate the meaning and mystery of God within the Australian cultural horizon. For this is still deeply mindful of the underdog, the little battlers, the poor little bastards that never had a chance. There is indeed 'a kingdom of no-thingness', to adapt Manning Clark's phrase, where we all belong: could it be that space of welcome that Jesus called the Kingdom of God, for which he gave his life? We invoke a limitless love as 'our Father', the mystery whose final meaning is to be 'everything to everyone', the one who is there, welcoming us into the home of a future in the house of many rooms.

The God of our Past

But any such reflection on human solidarity soon leads to a poignant silence. Given the relentless passing of time, how open can such a conversation really be? In an obvious sense, such a conversation is limited to those alive now: the conversation stops at the limits of death and in the presence of the unknown generations of those yet to be born. Dare we ask, do the defeated and the dead of past generations still have a voice in what it means to act humanly? Is amnesia really the condition for our present happiness? Are those on whose sufferings this present is built to be dispassionately consigned to oblivion: the dispossessed Aborigines, the convicts, the millions of hopeful immigrants, the pioneers who went out into the unknown? Have they simply served their purpose as the raw material for our development to this stage of 'the Australian way of life'? Is there any sense in which they belong with us in the fullness of the present as it tries to envisage a more human future? Have they simply died out of our future, or have they moved into it?

Not to wonder about answering such questions leaves our present all too naively immune to challenge. Was all that dying only for this? To possess the past only as a residue of defeat and death despairingly puts a circle around the present as the only significant historical moment. Is the unjust, violently structured repressed present the privileged place? At stake is the meaning of our human belonging. Is our hope an empty rhetoric when it speaks of leaving no one out? Were those who struggled for freedom, under the lash, loaded with the convicts ball and chain, bearing all the loneliness and the loss, simply lost? Is our history simply a series of euphoric instants in which all the pain and struggle is finally swallowed up in an uncaring present within an indifferent universe? Or is there something more, a space of mystery gathering all our history into itself?

About 75 per cent of Australians claim to live in the light of an answer to such questions. The silence has been broken. The Word has been uttered into the human conversation. Jesus Christ, crucified and risen, is the statement of God's irreversible self-involvement in our history.[23]   In the resurrection, the crucified one still bears the stigmata of the cross. Jesus is glorified as one whose blood was shed in solidarity with the poor, the hopeless, the historical failures, the condemned of the earth, with all the prophets and martyrs who went down with them. This Word of compassionate and ultimate love resists any foreclosure on the possibilities of human history. For the parable of the life, death and resurrection of Jesus is basic imaginative language of a truly social hope. In the light of the resurrection, the martyrs of our past are hailed as dying into the real future of the world. More generally all whom time and death have gathered out of our world still live in the region of our hope: 'I am the resurrection and the life; he who believes in me, though he die, yet shall he live' (Jn 11:25). The grain of wheat is isolated unless it die into the earth of human history, 'but if it dies, it bears much fruit' (Jn. 12:24).

In Christian terms…in that unique Divine embodiment for which we reserve the term Incarnation, Jesus lives from the first in a wholeness no mortal artist can sustain: He lives on the level of poetry, and thus shows us the way to that quality of life, which he calls the Kingdom. This Kingdom is Jesus' own poem and he embodies it fully, while revealing it as an aspect of God's poem…[24]

The God of our Imagination

If our most radical silence breathes the presence of the mystery invoked as 'our Father', our most hopeful conversation unfolds in the light of the Word that has been spoken. For it has been uttered into the darkness of our history. Despite the defiance of such hope, the darkness does remain. For it is still confronted with the defeat of the best among us, and with all that power of evil to crush human dignity and imprison freedom. At this point our imagination of what might be otherwise knows the temptation to give up. But it is precisely there that it can come to a new appreciation of what we call the Holy Spirit. This is the presence of God inspiring the new in human history. It inspires dreams for the old and visions for the young (Acts 2:17). On the one hand, this Spirit is not the 'spirit of slavery to fall back into fear'(Rom. 8:15), but that of being free with God,and free in a universe of limitless promise. For Christians, the Spirit is not an optimistic theory, but the energy of a universal love breathed into the hopeful heart (Rom. 5:5).

The ultimate: the mystery of God, Father, Son and Spirit; the mystery subverting anything we have too easily settled for, empowering the imagination to see the world otherwise.

Father: the all-welcoming mystery of our beginning and end, claiming us before any history we know, uniting us to one another before our different histories, welcoming us to the fullness of a future in a home of many rooms.

Son: God's membership in our suffering history; God bearing the burdens of the defeated, the forgotten; the crucified one suffering in solidarity with the poor whose only life is the nakedness of hope.

Spirit: the mystery indwelling the silence of our yearnings, unsettling us in these present times, inspiring visions and dreams of what we still might be, provoking us to a great risk of freedom to make this a place where we can flourish together.

God, then, is the silence in which we belong, the silence in which every voice is heard, all wounds are healed and all our times have a future, God of the 'no-thing', God of the centre, God of the common dish...

I find myself wondering in the end, whether such a God is the secret of our sense of humour, the irony that makes us mock those who want to forget the rest of us. Is this what Les Murray is getting at when he made the luminous remark:

> *The ability to laugh at venerated things, and at awesome and deadly things ... may in time prove to be one of Australia's greatest gifts to mankind. It is at bottom a spiritual laughter, a mirth that puts tragedy, futility and vanity back in their place. It was one of the things that led me back to Christianity.*[25]

The spiritual dimension is about how we imagine coming home to the true reality of Australia after some time of exile from the real things of our history. What is faith but the homing of the heart to that mystery involving us all? What is gospel but the telling of our life-stories and our national story as part of the autobiography of God. What really is the church but that part of the human community that knows, deeply knows, that there is healing still, that we are more than the dead weight of the past, that love and care and justice are the real stuff of life; that we are made for such life... If so, why not live now?

Our hitherto struggling or lost souls might now imagine things otherwise. We might be envisaged as running from our offices and school rooms, getting out of our suburban homes, forgetting out solemn posturing, to scurry down to the nearest beach and plunge back into the sea to start our history over again. We will be seen swimming out into the ocean's silence, into the simple bracing depths of things, stripped naked now of all disguises and fashions, washed clean of all cosmetics. Then, cleansed and refreshed, we are caught up in a huge dumper to be thumped unceremoniously onto the warm sand. And so dazed, yet with the triumph of escape, we get slowly to our feet, turn about us, and laughingly help drag the rest out of the pounding waves. And as our eyes turn to the shore, we make great gestures of greeting to those who are there long before us, those who have been quietly watching, astonished by the whole performance. Then, not without a sense of survival, not without a sense of the wonder at this place and at this grace of meeting in this moment of history, we begin slowly learning the new language of Australia's future.

---

1. Peter Malone, 'The Heart of Australia', *Compass Theology Review* 23, Summer 1988, p. 28.

2. See W. Bühlmann, *The Church of the Future*, Collins Dove, Melbourne, 1987.

3. See Miriam Rose Ungunmerr, *'Dadirri'*, *Compass Theology Review* 22, 1988, pp. 9–11; and in the same issue, D. Gondarra, 'Father, You gave us the Dreaming', pp. 6–8.

4. See Chapter 3.

5. See Chapter 2.

6. *Anthology...*, p. 180.

7. See also, Juanita Scari, 'Being Australian and Contemplative', *Compass Theology Review* 23, Summer 1988, pp. 32–34.

8. For these references, and a perceptive commentary, I am indebted to Lawrence Cross, 'The Precipice: an Image for contemporary Australian Theology?', *Discovering...*, pp. 105–121.

9. Harry S. Albinsky, 'Australia and the United States', *Australia...*, p. 404.

10. Patrick White, 'A Sense of Integrity', *Arena* 84, 1988, p. 99.

11. Murray Bail, *Homesickness*, Penguin, Melbourne, 1980, p. 201.

12. Patrick White, 'The Prodigal Son', *Australian Letters* 1/3, 1958, pp. 38–39.

13. Nicholas Jose, 'Cultural Identity', in *Australia...*, p. 314.

14. Jose, pp. 314–315.

15. Malone, p. 28.

16. Jose, *Australia...*, p. 315.

17. Les Murray, *Compass Theology Review* 23, Summer 1988, pp. 21–28.

18. Eric Voegelin, *Anamnesis*, G. Niemeyer (ed. and trans.), University of Notre Dame Press, 1978.

19. Donald Horne, 'Who Rules Australia?' *Australia...*, pp. 183–4.

20. Bernard Lonergan, *Method...*, p. 105.

21. See my *Trinity as Love. A Theology of the Christian God*, Michael Glazier, Wilmington, Del., 1989, especially the concluding chapters.

22. Les Murray, 'Some Religious Stuff I know about Australia', in *The Shape of Belief*, D. Harris, D. Hynd, D. Millikan (eds.), Lancer Books Anzea Publishers, 1982, p. 25.

23. For an inspiring presentation of the Christian spiritual journey, see Athol Gill, *Life on the Road. The Gospel Basis for a Messianic Lifestyle*, Lancer, Homebush, 1989.

24. Les Murray, *Embodiment and Incarnation*, Aquinas Library, Brisbane, 1987, p. 23.

25. Murray, 'Some Religious Stuff...', pp. 13–28.

A BODY BROKEN FOR A BROKEN PEOPLE

Frank Moloney SDB

The New Testament tells us that on the night before Jesus died, he celebrated a meal with his disciples. The event of this meal has been remembered in the life and liturgy of the Christian Church ever since.

In *A Body Broken for a Broken People,* Frank Moloney traces the basic traditions which record the words and actions of Jesus on that night. We discover that the early Church understood the Eucharist to be the place where people met the Lord despite their broken-ness.

Frank Moloney raises important questions for the Christian Church in this study. The reader is challenged to consider how welcome the broken are at the Eucharistic table in our contemporary Church.

Francis Moloney is an international biblical scholar. A Salesian priest, Frank lectures both in Australia and internationally.

ISBN 0 85924 892 5

FAITH IN SEARCH OF UNDERSTANDING

Charles Hill

For those many people interested in beginning a study of theology, here is a fitting introduction.

Human beings have an urge to make sense of the world. Christians endeavour to do this in the light of their belief. Hence Anselm's famous description of theology, 'faith in search of understanding.'

Here is a short, simply written accessible overview of theology. It describes what theology is and how it has been practised through the ages. The chapters are arranged in historical sequence to show how theology has been always developing.

Suggestions for relevant reading and exercises at the end of fourteen short chapters add to the book's usefulness. It is an ideal book for anyone starting out in this field.

Dr Charles Hill is a senior lecturer in the Religious Education Department of the Catholic College of Education, Sydney. He has studied in theology and scripture in the Lateran, Angelicum and Biblicum Universities. He is editor of the religious education journal *Word of Life*.

ISBN 0 85924 832 1

PRESSED DOWN AND FLOWING OVER

John Honner SJ

A book containing stories that can be read in many ways at different times. The stories are of one man's hope for the future and contain insights gained during the struggle for justice. New models are offered for unfolding and identifying Christian belief in day-to-day experience.

The meditations and lessons and stories gathered here offer a fresh and freeing outlook for followers of Jesus.

John Honner is at home in the inner city, the surf on the south coast of New South Wales, and in the bush. John was responsible for the publication of *Understanding Catholicism*, is rector at Jesuit Theological College in Melbourne and teaches at the United Faculty of Theology, Parkville, Melbourne.

ISBN 0 85924 835 6